Praise for *Ethics in Motion*

"I feel that *Ethics in Motion* is a must read for all CPA's. The examples provided in the book do an excellent job of demonstrating how one step in the wrong direction could lead down a path to consequences that nobody wants to face. The book is much more effective than our current professional requirements in addressing and provoking thought on ethical issues that we face as CPA's on a daily basis. *Ethics in Motion* would be a great tool to help young CPA's understand some of the dilemmas that they may face in the years to come and just as important it could be an excellent reminder and tool for those of us that have practiced for years to stay on the right path."
Steve Cleland, CPA, CFE / Beach Freeman Lim & Cleland, LLP

"Many of us cannot relate to Bernie Madoff or Bernie Ebbers or the crimes they committed. Justin Paperny, on the other hand, is someone we can identify with. He was a recent college graduate from a good family. He wanted to be a successful businessman. He wanted to make his parents proud. Is this the type of person who commits fraud? Apparently so. In an honest and an emotional story, we learn how a good guy went bad. Justin makes us believe that we are all capable of losing our way and teaches us the importance of staying on the right path. Unlike other books, this is not based on a theory...this is based on a reality. Let this convicted felon teach you about the real world that is full of pressure, opportunity and rationalization."
Rich Brody, Ph.D., CPA, CFE, CFF, FCPA,
Anderson School of Management, University of New Mexico

"Throughout the lively pages of *Ethics in Motion*, Justin Paperny not only depicts the devastating life-long consequences of wrong choices he made within the pressurized financial world, but also how he regained his moral compass, reaching out to help others acknowledge, reflect, and learn from similar actions. *Ethics in Motion* is a highly thoughtful, accessible and engaging collection of real situations in which people veer from internal ethical codes, and through humility and perseverance find their way back to their principles."
Nomi Prins, Author of *It Takes a Pillage*

"With revealing and informative openness, Justin Paperny describes mistakes he made which resulted in his rapid transition from successful young professional to serving time in jail. More than a cautionary tale, his reflections on what he learned, and his actions to get back on track, provide valuable insights for other young, ambitious professionals. Paperny also gathers a group of other real-world stories that shed light on how even very bright, talented people can lose their way, and work to find their way back."

John Ullmen, Ph.D., UCLA /Anderson School of Mgmt; co-author of *Who Wins Conflict? The Creative Alternative to Fight or Flight*

"Forget the shows on television. Take a walk through what really happens when someone is associated with fraud and deception. Then, prepare yourself for what the government will do when it investigates white-collar crime."

**Don Berecz (retired FBI) Director,
Fraud and Forensic Accounting Program
Georgia Southern University**

"The value of Justin's book to my MBA students is that it speaks to them—he doesn't fit their stereotypical image of a felon—they could be him, clean cut, well educated, and from an upper middle class family with loving parents. He did not start out to break the rules, but as his chapters tell, it was those seemingly innocent little choices he made each day that defined his character and ultimately his fate. These are stories of the intellect, the ego, being seduced by short-term gain and dismissive of long-term wisdom. For those who think "not me", read this book before Justin's experience becomes yours."

**Dennis Torres, Ph.D.; Pepperdine University,
Graziadio School of Business and Management**

"Instead of retelling the stories of Enron, WorldCom or other highly publicized frauds, Justin tells the stories of our neighbors, our friends, our co-workers who took that first step and paid the price. He tells these stories to warn us that none of us are immune to temptation and that first step can lead to a lifetime of regret."

**Tina Quinn, Ph.D., CPA; Professor of Accounting
Arkansas State University**

"We are all better than our worst acts. Most of us have a past, too; but not all of us have a memorialized past. Justin Paperny's *Ethics in Motion* is a superb example of a man who is accountable for his past by doing all he can to help others avoid the unforgiving mistakes which the best of us make when confronted with all the wrong circumstances."

Michael Sweig, Founder, The PCR Institute, and People with Criminal Records

"For individuals naive enough to believe they could never rationalize breaking the law, take a look your speedometer the next time you're speeding on an interstate highway. The difference between you and the ordinary people Justin profiles in this book is that your law violation has yet to result in a serious accident. His firsthand experience and powerful stories will enlighten students and managers that seemingly insignificant actions can introduce them to our legal system and accusations of illegal actions including wire, mail, or bank fraud."

Dr. Mark W. Lehman, CPA, CFE Associate Professor Emeritus of Accountancy Adkerson School of Accountancy Mississippi State University

Ethics in Motion

Justin M. Paperny

APS Publishing
PO Box 260461
Encino, California 91426

Ethics in Motion

Justin M. Paperny

APS Publishing
PO Box 260461
Encino, California 91426

With gratitude and affection, I dedicate this book to…

- ~ My parents, Bernard Paperny and Tallie Mayer, for their love, patience, and support. I remind myself, every day, how fortunate I am.
- ~ Michael Santos, my role model, for challenging me in federal prison to become better while reinforcing the importance of community, family, and responsibility.
- ~ Carole Santos, for giving as much support on the outside as Michael gave me on the inside.
- ~ Walt Pavlo, Jr, for helping me believe that felons have a place in the classroom, and for giving me Etika when the only thing I could offer in return was a thank you.
- ~ Sam Pompeo, for believing in me and giving me a second chance in business when so many others counted me out.
- ~ Brad Fullmer, my closest friend for more than 20 years, for reminding me that with hard work and discipline I can accomplish anything.

Justin M. Paperny
15 November 2010

**Other Books by
Justin M. Paperny**

Lessons From Prison

Ethics in Motion
Chapter Contents

Preface

Since I was a convicted felon, many would see an irony in my having authored a book on ethics. In fact, on 17 May 2010, I was summoned to appear before United States District Court Judge Stephen Wilson and the hearing reminded me of exactly who I was. I was not "a person" but "the subject" of that judicial proceeding, and the judge's refusal to consider me as a legitimate source for any type of ethics instruction became patently clear. I had a duty to prove otherwise.

The purpose of my court hearing concerned an unexpected tax refund of $31,908.04 that I received from the IRS. I was released from prison on 20 May 2009, but I remained under the close scrutiny of Mr. Isaiah Muro, a U.S. probation officer who was charged with the responsibility of supervising my release. When I called Mr. Muro to tell him of the surprise refund I had received, he told me that he would request a ruling from Judge Wilson to determine how much of the refund I could keep and how much I would have to surrender to pay toward the financial sanction that was a part of my sentence.

Since I walked out of prison 362 days before my court hearing, Mr. Muro had a relatively long history of supervising me. He understood the career I was striving to build and I found him supportive, firm but fair in his supervision. On account of my full compliance and cooperation with every request he made, Mr. Muro extended me a higher degree of liberty that I would have expected while working through the terms of my supervised release.

At 11.00 am sharp on the day of my hearing, everyone in the ornate courtroom rose to honor Judge Wilson as he entered. He sat in his high-backed chair on the dais, then began to review documents Mr. Muro submitted.

"I'm not sure why we're here." Judge Wilson readjusted himself in his seat as he cut to the heart of the matter. "I don't see how Paperny is entitled to any money. He doesn't have any rights."

Beong Soo-Kim represented the government and he responded to Judge Wilson. "The government is prepared to work out an equitable split with Mr. Paperny." I welcomed support from the prosecutor. He proposed that the judge allow me to retain some percentage of the funds to pay off personal debts, to print copies of *Lessons From Prison* (a book I wrote during my prison term), and to promote my career as a speaker on ethics.

Judge Wilson chuckled. "He is a felon!" His voice boomed from the bench. "We need a lot of things in this world, but a felon speaking on ethics is not one of them." The judge expressed contempt and doubts that my work could help anyone.

Joel Athey, the lawyer representing me, tried to argue on my behalf, describing efforts I've made to comply with my obligations and citing the six-figure amount I already had paid toward my commitment. The judge dismissed my lawyer's arguments, interrupting him in mid sentence by saying he didn't care about any efforts I had made to redeem myself. I was supposed to be broke, the judge said, to have nothing. As such, Judge Wilson ordered "the felon" to forfeit all funds other than the direct expenses associated with the preparation of my tax refund.

I understood Judge Wilson's dismissal of me as a human being. Encountering resistance was a price I expected to pay—over and over again—for the remainder of my life. Because of my acceptance, such demoralization would not deter my efforts to reconcile with society; one contribution I could make was sharing what I have learned.

To that end I not only relied on personal experiences, I also studied and contemplated the work of others. In reading the writings of Plato, the great Western philosopher who lived more than 2,500 years ago, I accepted that the most important task for an evolving society was to teach those in our communities. Every citizen had a role to play in passing along valuable lessons.

I respected scholars and societal leaders like Judge Wilson. They were well suited to dispense wisdom and to show by personal example how making the right kinds of decisions engendered self-respect, dignity, integrity, and the embodiment of the best our enlightened society could produce. Yet I had a role too, and that role was to show the consequences that could follow bad decisions. I was the yin to their yang—or vice versa.

News sources reported daily about well-educated individuals who began their lives with privilege and high expectations. As I once did they led careers of promise. Through my work I could help them detect and avoid the toxic combination of pressure, rationalization, and capacity that threatened to lead values astray. I once lacked an appreciation for the power of such threats and temptations. As news reports confirmed, the same went for countless numbers of white-collar offenders who never thought they would face disgrace as they sat beside attorneys at defendant's tables in courtrooms across America.

Despite my felony conviction (or perhaps because of it) I was positioned to show others how easily an ethical slide could lead down the chute of personal disaster and drop the transgressor into the iron jaws of the criminal justice system. This book would help to communicate that message.

In writing *Ethics in Motion* I thought about the time constraints of professionals and business students. They didn't need another volume on ethical theory to decorate bookshelves. With trade publications, news stories, textbooks, casebooks, and other literature professionals already had too much to read. Still, professionals and business students could benefit from insight into the decisions that resulted in demise for tens of thousands of professionals every year. I wrote this book to provide such insight.

The chapters that follow profile individuals who once led lives of distinction as professionals in the business community. I gathered their stories through consulting services I offered to people who were struggling through criminal prosecutions for mail fraud, wire fraud, tax fraud, tax evasion, bribery, and other white-collar type crimes. Despite their erstwhile perceptions of being morally upstanding citizens, they fudged on government forms; they participated in bribery or corruption schemes; they used the mail, the telephone, or the Internet to convey information that would mislead. Whereas they wanted to believe their actions did not represent more than indiscretions, their stories showed how such indiscretions derailed the promise of their lives. By neglecting attention to ethical development they made decisions that resulted in the loss of their careers, tearing apart their family's stability, reputation, and dignity. Their profiles showed how easily bad decisions could lead a person into our nation's growing population of felons.

Readers may work through the chapters sequentially, but since each chapter stands on its own, a linear reading isn't necessary. After describing my experiences, subsequent chapters show what I learned from others. They show how an executive decision to help a client, to advance the firm's business, to close a deal, or to make things right resulted in their becoming targets of criminal prosecutions. Such profiles, I hope, will help those in my audience connect the dots. I want them to understand why it's not enough "to know" that path to an ethical life. By passing along what I have learned I offer compelling reasons that show why individuals should commit to walking that path every day, with every decision in their personal lives and in their careers. They were lessons I learned the hard way.

Justin M. Paperny
15 November 2010

*To make no mistakes is not in the power of
man; but from their errors and mistakes the
wise and good learn wisdom for the future.*
~ Plutarch

Chapter One
Discovering Ethics in Motion

My name is Justin Paperny. On 20 May 2009, I was released from the federal prison camp in Taft, California. I was 34 years old, a graduate of the University of Southern California, and a former stockbroker who built my career at Merrill Lynch, Bear Stearns, and UBS. But as I carried out my two cardboard boxes of belongings through prison doors to meet my mother, Tallie, I understood that a felony conviction would tarnish my résumé forever. What was I going to do with the lessons I learned?

My mother greeted me with her arms wide open, tears rolling down her cheeks. I had pleaded guilty to a single count of violating securities laws, and as a sanction, I served 400 days in prison. During that year I worked to atone, preparing myself to live as a contributing citizen. I wanted to emerge with insight and perspective that might help expiate the shame and guilt weighing upon my shoulders. Somehow, I wanted to prove worthy of the embrace I was about to receive.

While readjusting through my first year after returning to society, I had ample time to continue a process of looking inward and outward. That introspection served as a useful strategy to carry me through the indignities of imprisonment. Although I would never again live in the midst of 500 confined felons, I would always live as a part of a larger community. To ensure that I would never put the privilege of my liberty in jeopardy again—and to work toward redeeming my reputation—I made a commitment to live an ethical life. That commitment necessitated my study of ethics.

My motivations were more pragmatic than theoretical. I was not interested in building a new career as a scholar of philosophy, but I learned from the writings of Aristotle, Immanuel Kant, and John Stuart Mill. These writings helped me interpret the motivations that led to my crime. They also helped me put into context what I learned from others whose lapses in ethics led to problems in their careers, their personal lives, and sometimes, their challenges with the criminal justice system.

As a prisoner I was surrounded with men who could serve as case studies for courses on the importance of ethical decision-making. Like me, the men were reared in homes and communities that nurtured and prepared them for leadership. They were educated in America's best universities and led careers of distinction in law, medicine, finance, politics, and business. I introduce some of those men in the pages that follow. In sharing what I learned from them, readers will see that neither background nor successes protect against the lasting perils that follow an inattention to ethics.

Besides learning from men who sat beside me in federal prison, I drew lessons from contemporary figures who made decisions that have tarnished their standing in society. Like millions of fans around the world, for example, I was saddened in the fall of 2009 when headlines broke about Tiger Woods. Tiger and I were about the same age, yet for years I admired him from afar as an individual of the highest caliber. In Tiger I saw a commitment to personal excellence, a work ethic and discipline that struck me as the perfect example for which all individuals should strive. Success seemed his on every level. Tiger was the indisputable leader of his profession, and corporations from around the globe paid tens of millions to associate their brands to his reputation. The surface glimpses of his life suggested that Tiger enjoyed the loving warmth of a model family, with his striking wife and two adorable children.

Mere hours after Tiger confessed to infidelity, however, some of his most public sponsors wanted their association with him to disappear. *The New York Times* reported Accenture, the worldwide consulting firm, had been using Tiger in 83 percent of the company's ads. The company's ad campaign had been about high performance, but with Tiger's confession to infidelity in his personal life, Accenture no longer recognized Tiger as a metaphor for high performance.

Accenture's ads featuring Tiger—crouching on the green, studying a golf balls trajectory, him peering into the distance through foreboding dark clouds, him high stepping through tall grass beside a caption about the "road to high performance" not always being paved—no longer applied. It wasn't Tiger's performance as a golfer that led to the loss of his reputation. Rather, confessions about his personal life revealed flaws that misrepresented him as a pillar of virtue. Accenture spent $50 million in advertising a year to cultivate an image that defined good character, including ideals like honesty, loyalty, trustworthiness, and decency. After Tiger's confession, executives at Accenture concluded that Tiger's behavior did not represent such virtues.

As I read the seemingly endless coverage of Tiger Woods, I thought about how a man who had been blessed with so much apparent success could make decisions that imperiled an identity others valued so highly. His decisions may not have crossed criminal boundaries, but from them I could draw lessons in ethics, just as I learned from the writings of philosophy, and just as I learned from the high-level professionals who revealed their stories to me.

Our society reveres professional athletes like Tiger Woods, but I'm convinced that we should look beyond the celebrity arena to find those role models who embody the principles of an ethical life. Those who give themselves generously to the making of a better society, perhaps surprisingly, are those who give without concern for spotlights on their own stardom. I'm talking about people who work to shape good character, like teachers and coaches. I knew many such community builders as I was growing from childhood, through adolescence, and into my early adulthood.

As a youngster baseball defined me. From my first little league coach, Jack Gilardi, I learned about discipline, good sportsmanship, and leadership. As a coach, his only concern was in helping each of us on the team reach our highest potential. The virtues coach Gilardi and others encouraged became an integral part of my life through my continuing participation on baseball teams at Montclair Prep and at USC, where the value of teamwork was instilled in every player. Yet as has been the unfortunate case with so many others, those values and characteristics of good citizenship became less important with graduation from academia and advancement into the professional world.

Icons from my beloved sport of baseball, as another example, have rocked the sports world with admissions that they were not worthy of admiration as role models. I grew up inspired by athletes like Mark McGwire, a player who smashed homeruns out of ballparks season after season, breaking records that others said couldn't be broken. Yet in early 2010, I shook my head sadly while watching him offer a tearful apology to baseball fans for his lying and cheating.

Mark McGwire enjoyed the glory of being an outstanding athlete from his first little league at bat, when

Chapter One

he homered to loud applause. His hitting skill and mastery of the game accelerated with every season, as numerous awards evidenced. As happened with me, however, at some point Mark McGuire's core values deteriorated. His apology for breaking rules, and then lying to cover up his dishonesty, brought painful reminders of my own character weaknesses; in my case those weaknesses resulted in an ethical slide that eventually crossed the line into criminality. The reminder prompted questions about the role that societal leaders have in conveying the importance of ethical values.

How do we pass along the importance of ethical values to generations of future leaders? When I was a university student, professors would require dense reading in ethical theories, but my youthful arrogance blocked my ability to learn from theoretical perspectives. Since then, time and experience have convinced me that I should have given more attention to the lessons presented. After watching two of my heroes from sports fall because of a disregard for ethical decision making—and after all I learned during my year in federal prison—I decided to take another look at what those philosophers wrote about and consider what my university professors had hoped I would learn.

In reading Immanuel Kant again, I was reminded of his much acclaimed categorical imperative. Essentially, I understood Kant's philosophy on ethics as indicating a moral code existed, and each of us as fellow human beings had a duty to act in accordance with that morality. I must have been bored or too lacking in focus to grasp Kant's brilliance, because his message that the moral code required us to refrain from lying, cheating, or stealing didn't strike me as being particularly profound or illuminating. I knew it all.

It may have been the heavy, scholarly language of Kant that blocked me from receiving his message during my younger years. While in college, I didn't consider the possibility that circumstances would ever change to the point that I could engage in such acts. In my mind, the possibility didn't exist that I would face dilemmas or temptations that would change the core of who I was as a man. Having grown up in Encino, an affluent suburb of Los Angeles, no one was going to categorize me as being "at-risk," and of course I didn't see myself as being without privileges.

With my expectations that I had a rightful place in society, Kant's lessons on the moral imperative didn't seem to tell me anything I didn't already know—at least that's one reason I may have tuned out when I was in college. I understood the difference between right and wrong, but knowledge alone was insufficient—in my case—to appreciate the value of ethical training.

Another philosopher my professors introduced me to was John Stuart Mill, a father of utilitarianism. As I understood his theory, people could calculate an ethical value by measuring what gave the greatest good to the greatest number. I found it even easier to tune out the theory of utilitarianism. The greatest good for the greatest number? Come on! I understood enough about right and wrong, I thought, that I wouldn't need to waste time rationalizing my decision making with such esoteric concepts.

The philosopher who made the most sense to me with regard to teaching ethics was Aristotle. He did not encourage the thinking about moral codes or calculating what was good for the most people, but instead reduced the ethical lesson to the individual, making it easier to grasp. Aristotle famously said moral excellence comes about as a result of habit, suggesting that what really counted was the

11

cultivation of good character. An individual had to look within, and in so doing, commit daily to cultivating virtues that included honesty, loyalty, sincerity, integrity, and so forth. In so doing, the good life would follow. What was good for the individual was good for the community.

When I left USC, I thought I understood Aristotle's lesson as well as I understood how to breathe. A version of this philosophy had been ingrained in me since childhood by all of my teachers and coaches and other role models. Later, however, when I left the university and moved into the professional world, challenges or dilemmas began to present themselves that would test my true understanding of Aristotle's message. And in those tests, I was found wanting. Whereas I didn't need to think about breathing, I seemed to have forgotten Aristotle's formula. Namely, living an ethical life required continuous cultivation and nurturing of virtues; it also required a commitment to personal excellence.

I read an amusing quote attributed to Oscar Wilde that highlighted the need for individuals to hone virtues. Wilde said that he "could resist anything except temptation." So how does a man resist temptation? The Bible taught that temptation was as old as man, first revealed in the book of Genesis, with Eve's bite of the apple. Temptation, I suspect, led Tiger Woods to betray his family, and temptation urged Mark McGwire to cheat in pursuit of greatness. In my case, temptation was the root cause of my breaking the law. A continuous honing of virtues would have made each of us less susceptible to temptation.

I may not personally know Tiger Woods or Mark McGwire, but I suspect that I shared at least one thing in common with both men. Each of us believed we understood "the moral code" that Kant wrote about. We also understood that neither lying nor cheating nor stealing were actions consistent with what would lead to the greatest good for the greatest number. What we didn't appreciate, however, was Aristotle's admonition that living "the good life" required a continuous cultivation of virtues and that cultivation would lead to good character.

Knowing right from wrong alone didn't endow us with the strength to confront all challenges, dilemmas, or temptations that we faced in life. Only the cultivation of a personal ethical code could provide such strength. Like an athlete or performing artist must never relent with practice, the individual who aspired to excellence had to introspect, continuously questioning his level of commitment to developing the virtues of good character. I understood that principle in sports.

As a young athlete I practiced my sport every day. I had an inherent understanding that to improve my skills as a ballplayer, I needed constant conditioning, individually through fitness training and diet, and by joining the team for regular drills on fundamentals of the game. It wasn't that we were learning anything new about baseball, but we all understood that practice would make us better.

Advancing in the professional arena was different. I presented my academic credentials, then I sat for licensing examinations that would certify my competence as a financial professional. Yet once my career began my values changed, with the need for personal development going to the wayside. Instead, a short-sighted craving for personal advancement motivated me, and earnings rather than excellence became my measuring rod for success.

My career as a stockbroker at Merrill Lynch, Bear Stearns, and UBS introduced me to the Hobbesian theory of every man being out for himself. Each of those storied Wall Street firms kept stacks of rarely used binders stuffed with laminated pages complete with platitudes in big bold fonts that highlighted the firm's commitment to the highest ethical standards. In practice and in corporate culture, the message differed. It felt more like an atmosphere from the Chicago School of Economics where Milton Friedman taught, with the only responsibility of business being to make money.

I misunderstood Friedman's lessons on supply-side economics, and what I misunderstood contributed to an incremental abandonment of social responsibility; that abandonment brought my demise. Within a few years of mentorship under brokers who instructed me on prospering as a stockbroker, the lessons Coach Gilardi began instilling in me when I was a little leaguer began to fade. In the place of honesty, integrity, and trustworthiness, I developed avarice, ambition, and arrogance. My new mentors, men who worked alongside me as stockbrokers taught me how to churn accounts and select investments that would enhance commissions instead of client returns. I was impressionable and a "pleaser," going along with the fellas and the culture of fast money.

Those abuses of discretion began my incremental slide to ethical indifference. In time, that indifference led to a willful disregard of clear evidence that should have prompted me to notify superiors and law enforcement authorities about a potential fraud. Instead, I looked the other way so as not to interrupt the steady flow of six-figure commissions.

The fraud that led to my conviction for violating a provision of securities law concerned my oversight of a hedge fund. The manager who ran the hedge fund had lost millions of dollars in investor funds through inappropriate speculations. I had reason to suspect wrongdoing, or that something was awry with the hedge fund because it continued to attract new deposits despite a steady record of losses.

My willful ignorance was bad enough, but self-preservation later set in. Despite my suspicions of fraud, I encouraged the trading to continue. Instead of using my discretion as a force for good to protect investor assets, I schemed with my colleagues and superiors at UBS to protect us from potential liability. Later, an investor in the hedge fund confronted me with questions, and in so doing, the investor presented brokerage account statements that I could tell at a glance were forgeries. Instead of exposing what I then knew to be a crime, I ignored the clear evidence of fraud by the hedge fund manager. Had I cultivated a stronger ethical core, embraced individual responsibility, developed a sense of integrity, I would have had the courage to act appropriately. I'm ashamed to admit that after only five years into my career, I had abandoned anything but lip service to the cultivation and development of a strong ethical center. As such, I remained silent to the fraud, thereby making me a part of the crime and ultimately leading to my disgrace; imprisonment soon followed.

In struggling with my troubled conscience, reflecting on how my sense of morals deteriorated, and recognizing the vulnerabilities other citizens had to this same fate, I contemplated whether anyone could teach courses that would instill morality. I came to the conclusion that teaching could never be enough. Like most college students, I had studied the requisite courses. Certainly, I understood the difference between right and wrong. What I needed was the courage to make the right decisions and to derive a sense of personal fulfillment—or identity—from my strong ethical commitments. More than being taught, that courage to act (courage that came from a strong ethical core) needed to be honed, practiced, and constantly cultivated.

When businesses produce binders of ethical policies, they strike me as adhering to a version of the

Kantian "moral imperative," presenting a code of behavior that employees should follow. The problem that existed at Merrill Lynch, Bear Stearns, and UBS, were that the culture trumped the code. From my experience as a financial professional, and from what I learned through the stories of other white-collar offenders I've met, I've become convinced that rather than publishing moral codes (that few employees follow), businesses could serve employees, their communities, and their shareholders better by encouraging individuals to develop their personal virtues and integrity. Such investments would do far more to enhance corporate policy than clichés. I had such encouragements while being raised in the family home.

My parents, Tallie and Bernie, did their best to develop a sense of virtue and decency in my brother Todd and me. They not only explained to us that we were part of a larger community, but they devised lessons that would teach us the value of contribution. During the holiday season, I remember Tallie instructing me to choose one of the Hanukkah gifts I received and give it to another child who was less fortunate that I was. "In helping others," she would tell me, "you strengthen your community, and in strengthening your community, you strengthen each of us, including yourself."

Those were the kinds of moral exercises that ceased to become a part of my life when I joined the professional world of money management. Instead of working to build a stronger community, I focused exclusively on earning higher commissions. Since the higher commissions I earned simultaneously meant higher profits (in the short term) for my employers, the businesses that employed me were silent as to the patterns of deceit being sewn to generate those results.

My consideration of the corporate cultures that groomed me piqued a curiosity on whether there might be better ways to foster an ethical environment. That curiosity led me to the writings of Professor Herant Katchadourian, of Stanford University, who wrote about concepts of shame and guilt. Dr. Katchadourian's work contrasted aspects of our Western culture—where we valued individualism— with Eastern cultures that placed more emphasis on community. In our focus to advance personally, those of us in the West could come to feel less empathy or responsibility for others—especially when we failed to cultivate a strong ethical core.

In the West, we looked out for ourselves and we expected others to do the same. Asian cultures, I learned from reading Dr. Katchadourian's work was based on a different premise. Instead of the individual, the Asian cultures focused on ensuring harmony in relationships, on keeping the integrity of the whole. Because they focused on preserving the community, the motivations and incentives were for groups to grow, succeed, and prosper; instead of codes that instructed individuals on avoiding wrong behaviors, the Asian cultures placed more emphasis on doing what was right over the long term for the group. People, then, created their identities by how well they fit into the group, whether it was the family, the business community, or society.

Since Aristotle was from Greece, I always thought of him as a Western philosopher. In reading about Aristotle's recipe for building greater communities, however, I recognized the same wisdom that Asian cultures embraced. Namely, by cultivating character in the individual—encouraging every member of the group to develop the highest sense of personal integrity—great and lasting relationships followed.

Those teachings from both East and West instructed that building greatness in any relationship required continuous personal investment. Prohibitive rules or principles—such as those in the "ethics binders" that many corporations published—would not foster ethical environments, or communities, as well as individual commitments to practice and cultivate a strong ethical center.

Developing a strong ethical core wasn't like developing the competence to pass a history examination. Developing ethics required more than reading books or memorizing facts. Knowing right from wrong would never be enough. In my case, I knew it was wrong to allow a hedge fund manager to deceive his investors; Tiger Woods knew it was wrong to betray his commitment to his family; and Mark McGwire knew it was wrong to break rules and to lie about his actions.

We knew right from wrong. The roots of our failure were not knowledge of right and wrong, but in not recognizing that building strong ethical centers required constant practice, attention, and personal investment to cultivate character. This recipe of focusing on individual responsibility applied to building great marriages; rearing successful families; leading successful, fulfilling careers; building strong societies; and to experiencing happiness.

My coaches understood that principle. From my years in little league through my time at USC, my baseball coaches emphasized the importance of practice. I could read all the books in the world about how to stop a grounder or how to swing a bat, but becoming the best ballplayer possible required practice, day after day, season after season. The day I stopped practicing was the day my hand-eye coordination and skills would begin to deteriorate. Without that hand-eye coordination and skills, my ability to play the game suffered.

In that way, ethical training was like athletic training. A person could train hard one season, but the day he stopped would be the day his fitness and strength would atrophy. The great athlete in college could easily put on weight and fall into patterns of laziness if he stopped training. I know. Similarly, the person who practiced honesty, loyalty, and sincerity through their early years (and who thinks those virtues would always be with him), could deteriorate into a dishonest financial professional, an unfaithful husband, and a rule-breaking liar. When we cease to cultivate a strong ethical center, each of us becomes vulnerable to the baseness we detest and rightfully attribute to an inferior character. Without character, we lessen our abilities to use discretion appropriately, to make good judgments, to build great relationships and communities.

Countless books interpret the teachings of the world's great philosophers and ethicists. In my quest to overcome the character flaws that led to my shame and imprisonment, I've read a fair share of those books. Besides learning that an inattention to ethics leads to an inferior character, I also learned that through renewed attention to the subject, individuals could take steps to improve. Just like the out-of-shape individual could exercise his way back toward improved physical fitness, a person who once made bad decisions could introspect, look inward and outward to begin cultivating the traits that in time would restore good character.

As individuals need regular exercise to maintain physical fitness levels, individuals need exercise to nurture good-character attributes. In thinking about how I could help an individual nurture good character attributes, I thought about what would have helped me. More lessons on philosophical theories may have cured insomnia, but I don't think more lectures on rules, codes, or right and wrong would have held my interest—especially since I worked in a culture that would wink at violations of such rules and codes so long as profits and commissions flowed.

More pragmatic lessons, on the other hand, could have inspired me to cultivate the good character necessary to make ethical decisions. If I understood that every individual—even those who came from privilege—was vulnerable to disastrous consequences that frequently followed judgments made from an inferior character, I'd like to think that I could have done better, that I would have understood more about my need to cultivate character. As Professor Jana Craft from St. Mary's University taught, I could train to make values-based decisions. One way of furthering such training was through exposure to stories from contemporary society that described people from my social, educational, and economic background. Had I learned about consequences that followed the ethical slide of others, I would have been more alert of the need to guard my commitment to an ethical code vigilantly. Such an investment would have made me a better person, a better employee, a better citizen.

I cannot undo the bad decisions I made in my early 20's, when the beginning of my career initiated an ethical slide. All I can do now is work to become better. That effort begins with my daily commitment to personal responsibility and the cultivation of good character. This ongoing exercise requires that I look inward and outward pursuing a course that will instill the virtues of honesty, loyalty, sincerity, temperance, and other virtues that will contribute to making me a better man so I can contribute to the making of a better community and a better overall society.

As a roadmap to keep me on course, I've adopted a simple diagram from the Kellogg Foundation.

RESOURCES→ACTIVITIES→ OUTPUTS→OUTCOMES→ IMPACT

By following the diagram, I not only work on strengthening my own character, but I also use what I've learned to contribute to the lives of others as part of my looking inward and outward.

—In my **RESOURCES** block I consider what I have to offer. I'm a college graduate, a former stockbroker, and a former federal prisoner. I am ashamed to have experienced every aspect of the criminal justice system, but I've learned from the humiliating process as well as from listening to others.

—In my **ACTIVITIES** block I identify steps to put my resources to their highest potential use. Since experience is my resource, I use it to gather stories that show the consequences following ethical slides.

—In my **OUTPUTS** block I track the various ways I can convert the stories into teachable lessons, providing descriptions, commentary, and analysis for others.

—In my **OUTCOMES** block I evaluate whether my writings, speeches, and consultations inspire those in my audience to cultivate stronger ethical centers that become intrinsic to their lives and become driving forces for their success.

—In my **IMPACT** block I ensure that the body of work I create strengthens my individual responsibility to lead an ethical life and encourages others to do the same.

The stories that follow describe lessons I've learned from others. Their ethical slides led to experiences with the criminal justice system and heavy sanctions that followed bad decisions. I hope readers find as much value in these stories as I have found in writing them. Each lesson strengthens my commitment to practice ethics in motion.

Chapter One Questions

- Use the Kellogg diagram to show deliberate steps you are taking in one of your life's activities.

  1. Resources

  2. Activities

  3. Outputs

  4. Outcomes

  5. Impact

Chapter Two
Cultivating Character

Although I have never abused alcohol or any other type of substance, I've admired the 12-step treatment programs I've read about. They were effective in helping millions of people straighten out their lives because those programs emphasized the importance of personal responsibility and continuous self-awareness.

In reading about the 12-step programs I recognized a relationship to Aristotle's teachings on the need for introspection. A pattern existed that any of us could follow to become better human beings, and by becoming better human beings we all contribute to building better relationships, better careers, and better communities. With my return to society, I looked forward to my own daily introspection that would continue my ethical training and further my commitment to leading a values-centered life.

Like the recovering alcoholic understood that maintaining sobriety required abstinence from the consumption of alcohol, I understood that redeeming myself and working toward becoming a person of good character would require a day-by-day effort for the rest of my life. Prison may not have "saved" my life, but the loss of my liberty certainly made me realize the necessity of ensuring that the decisions I made and the activities I pursued were in harmony with the values I held.

Without that balance, I made decisions that brought painful consequences. While incarcerated, for example, I suffered mightily when I heard of the death of my dog, Honey My heart ached with the reality that decisions I had made meant that I missed the last months of her life and that I would never see her wagging tail again. Besides losing my dog, I never missed freedom as much as I did on 22 January 2009 the day that Sunny, my sister-in-law, brought my niece Clover into this world. I should have been present to celebrate my niece's birth, and those irretrievable losses would ensure that I never made another decision that would disregard my responsibility to family and good citizenship.

As I was sitting in a restaurant, holding my niece for the first time and looking into her big blue eyes that were filled with curiosity, enjoying the loving warmth from family and friends who welcomed me home, I wondered why it took a journey through prison for me to realize that I could never take freedom for granted. I lost nearly all of my material belongings and net worth due to my struggles with the criminal justice system, but in going through it I came to appreciate family, community, and reputation much more. I was 34 and resuming life with clouds of six-figure debt hanging over me, but somehow, the clarity of values brought self-confidence, inner peace, and a certainty of my place in the world. In striving to become better, and in sharing the lessons I learned, I was going to become a force for good.

Roger Ewing opened an opportunity to test my usefulness in society as a force for good. Together with his partner, Ernie Wish, Roger presided over the distinguished Sotheby's real estate office in Calabasas, an affluent suburb of Los Angeles. Sotheby's employed a sales force of more than 125 highly trained sales professionals. Despite my having been released from federal prison, Roger agreed to hire me. When considering my request for work, Roger said that he understood the economy was tight and that market conditions required everyone in the upscale office to work harder for less compensation. He also understood that in hiring me, Roger would be subjecting everyone in his office to the inconveniences presented by federal authorities who were supervising my conditional release to society. Despite the intrusions that would come with hiring a felon, Roger told me that on account of my efforts to atone for the crimes that led to my imprisonment and the daily commitment I was making to society, he respected me. Such words had more value to me than I knew how to describe and I intended to prove worthy of his trust.

Rather than hiring me to sell mansions to the stars, I came on in a supportive role, contributing to the company's newsletters and blogs. The opportunity allowed me to earn a modest income while working to build my new career speaking to audiences about the importance of ethics and consulting for business people who encountered troubles with the criminal justice system. In early August, three months after my return to society, I presented my first corporate ethics speech to the sales staff at Sotheby's.

The irony of my standing before the group as a convicted felon was not lost on me. I told the group about my prior career as a stockbroker and I shared with them how management once compelled my colleagues and me to attend continuing education courses—including some on ethics. While I sat through such lectures on corporate compliance, I told my audience, I used to tune out, certain that I understood about right and wrong. I didn't think I needed others to tell me about rules that governed my profession.

Although I did not want to listen to lectures on rules or codes of conduct, I would have been well advised to learn more about why I should have cultivated virtues that constituted good character. It was my disregard for, my dismissal of, my indifference to such virtues, I explained to my audience, that resulted in my exchanging designer suits and million dollar commissions for prison jumpsuits and a

25

steel rack next to a tattooed man who identified himself as Big Homie.

A sense of entitlement crept up on me after I left the University and became more immersed in the go-go-go culture of Wall Street. It was always the next deal that motivated me, the higher commissions, the perceived prestige that came with rapid advancement. In my insatiable pursuit of more external validations, I felt less inclined to appreciate the peace and wholeness that only came with a strong inner core.

In time my focus on short-term rewards led to the rotting of my inner core, rendering me more and more vulnerable to consequences that conspired together to ruin my life. First there was an inattention to my physical fitness. My excuse was that advancing in my career required long hours. I ate fast food and neglected exercise. Instead of making adjustments, I accepted my expanding waistline and pudginess as an inevitable consequence of growing older. That was the beginning of my inattention to the importance of self-discipline, and in time, I told my audience, what began with a lack of physical training deteriorated into a lack of integrity training.

Instead of embracing the virtues of humility, balance, and discipline, a kind of envy took root inside of me. I was young, in my mid-twenties, single, and earning commission checks that sometimes reached six figures levels in a single month as a stockbroker. Yet rather than living in gratitude for such monetary rewards (as distinguished from success), I coveted what others had. Men and women in the same office appeared to work less and earn more. Why wasn't I bringing in bigger numbers? I felt cheated, under appreciated. With self-delusions of entitlement, I lacked both perspective and clarity.

As my inattention to the crucial need for introspection and cultivating character became more pronounced, a selfishness that I didn't recognize began to define who I was. I hated my life and my career. I hated the early mornings. I hated fielding phone calls to clients that I felt were undeserving of my attention. I zoned out, staring at golf tournaments on television or playing games of online chess. I lost interest in the value of nurturing close personal relationships. Instead, a pathetic self-pity over why I wasn't receiving the recognition I deserved rendered me incapable of realizing how out of balance my values had become. Perhaps I didn't abuse alcohol, but I was like the drunk who couldn't comprehend why everyone was saying he had a drinking problem. Denial, an inattention to the wreck of a man I had become, plagued me.

I could see that many of the sales professionals in my audience identified with the state of mind that I described. They may not have suffered from similar character weaknesses, but they saw such vice in others. For some reason, it was always easier for us to see flaws in others. Introspection, on the other hand—looking inward and evaluating whether our thoughts, words, and actions synchronized with the professional images we wanted to portray, with the spouses or parents or citizens we wanted to be—required discipline. In my case, I told the group, that lack of discipline led to a weakening of my commitment to ethics and morality.

I told those in my audience how moral faults and failings made it easier to cross a line that would later lead to my being targeted by the criminal justice system. I justified lies that I knew would result in losses to investors. That was wrong on so many levels. Rules of my professions prohibited such lies. Yet I could justify my actions by convincing myself that such lies were part of the professional culture, that everyone did it. Although the law did not permit deceit that I was in a position to perpetuate, I felt entitled to the money that the lies I told would generate. For those lies, I was convicted of securities fraud—and rightly so.

Chapter Two

The coldness of concrete and steel convinced me that I had to change. While lying on a prison rack I began to see how my life had fallen apart. It wasn't because of my criminal conviction, but because I had failed to cultivate ethical principles. Temptations of money, power, lust, and other corrupting forces were ubiquitous in our society. By disregarding my ethical core—meaning that I diminished the inherent values of integrity, discipline, balance, humility, and so forth—I rendered myself less and less capable of defending against ever-present temptations. By the time I concluded my prison term, I told those in my audience, just as I knew that I would never stop brushing my teeth, I knew that I would never again ignore the necessity of working to build a better inner character.

When I concluded the prepared portion of my presentation for the audience at Sotheby's I invited questions. Besides the many understandable questions about what prison was like, I responded to several questions inquiring about specific changes I made to cultivate character.

For me the changes were all-encompassing, I told the group. After leaving USC I made the mistake of ignoring good books, but in prison I read extensively. In reading various anthologies of philosophy, I developed my appreciation for Aristotle that continues to grow. His message was that when we continuously worked to improve the self, we simultaneously worked to improve our communities. In neglecting that "continuing improvement of the self," I had harmed our community.

Besides relying upon the writings of Aristotle, I found inspiration in Rodin's sculpture of *The Self Made Man*. To improve the self, I pledged to work every day on improving my fitness, my knowledge, and my inner peace as well as my balance.

I began exercising daily by running long distances. That time alone, as I ran through the hills of Pacific

Palisades, with eucalyptus trees scenting the air, or alongside the beaches of Southern California, breathing in the elements, I felt at one with nature. The rhythmic, soothing sound of my steps crunching the gravel was all I heard. While the exercise improved my fitness, the tranquility brought an hour or two away from iPhones, e-mails, and phone calls that I could count on every day to evaluate decisions and activities.

Instead of narcotizing myself with distractions from an iPod, I welcomed exercise time to examine the motives behind my decisions. Was I reading literature that would expand my knowledge? Was I honest and forthright in all of my relationships or exchanges with others? Was I appreciative of my blessings? Was I contributing to my community by adding value to the lives of others? Such introspections, or self-questioning, helped me stay on course; as exercise would improve my physical fitness, contemplations would help me cultivate character.

I appreciated the opportunity Roger Ewing opened for me to speak at Sotheby's and the practice served me well. Over the next several months I spoke to much larger audiences in universities and corporate settings from coast to coast. The purpose of my work was to illustrate ways that people who considered themselves good, or ethical, could fall vulnerable to making decisions if their values fell out of whack. Such decisions jeopardized stability for individuals, for the businesses that employed them, and for the economy. I considered it my duty to work toward reducing white-collar crime, and I could do that by sharing what I've learned. Practical lessons on ethics could remind people that efforts to cultivate character should be ongoing.

Sharing my experiences with university and corporate audiences was in some ways reaffirming. In literature for Alcoholics Anonymous I read that those who participated in and attended regular meetings reaffirmed their commitment to sobriety; they also developed support by telling their stories. I felt certain that I would root all of my future thoughts, words, and actions in honesty and integrity, but sharing my story was cathartic. Each presentation represented a strengthening of my ethical core, furthering my commitment to lead a values-based life. On top of that, in relating what I learned from ethical theorists to the real, day-to-day challenges of the workforce, I could offer those in my audience practical insight. They would use it, I hoped, to stay true to the principles of good behavior and avoid the temptations that frequently lead to white-collar crime.

In continuing my education on what drives good people into white-collar crime, I learned from the writings of Jim Ratley, the president of the Certified Fraud Examiners. He consulted for businesses that invested in white-collar crime prevention programs. Mr. Ratley pointed out that those who transmogrified from good corporate citizen to white-collar criminal had the trifecta of toxic combinations: pressure (they needed the money); capacity (they were in a position to commit fraud); and rationalization (they could explain why they were entitled to the ill-gotten fruits they coveted).

Walt Pavlo was another business consultant (and mentor of mine) who worked assiduously to explain motivations that led to fraud. Mr. Pavlo called pressure, capacity, and rationalization components of the fraud triangle. I could identify with such theories because of personal experience. But as my business expanded to include consulting with business or legal professionals who faced struggles with the criminal justice system, I saw how those who neglected the need to train their ethical cores were most vulnerable to the perils presented by "the fraud triangle."

Generally speaking, the business professionals who contacted me for advice on how to emerge from their troubles with the law understood right from wrong. They considered themselves good people, ethical. They would not have been able to imagine themselves using a gun or participating in any type of street-level crime. Yet in disregarding the need to cultivate strong ethical centers, they succumbed to temptations of participating in vulpine acts of deceit.

The people who contacted me for consulting services held positions that gave them capacity to respond to their perceived pressures with fraud. In their minds they could rationalize their actions. Those actions led to criminal charges, and it became my job to help them find their way back.

I share what I learned from those white-collars offenders in an effort to expand the literature on ethics. I want those in the business community (and those who study in preparation to join the business community) to have more information than that contained in corporate compliance binders; unfortunately, those binders that were rarely consulted did nothing more than gather dust in business offices across America. Perhaps stories of real people who once held positions of trust in big business, small business, or professional services—but now faced charges for white-collar crime—would convince more professionals of the need to introspect, to cultivate character and strong ethical cores, as Aristotle advised.

Chapter Two Questions

1. Identify the five highest values of your life in ascending order.

2. Describe how your daily actions, your relationships, your decisions relate to each of those values.

3. Describe the level of consistency between your proclaimed values with your actions, relationships, and decisions.

Chapter Three
Joshua the CFO

Joshua contacted me after searching for information on the Web that would help him understand what to expect in federal prison. Like most white-collar offenders, he never envisioned the possibility that he would encounter problems with the law.

"I've never known anyone who has even been arrested," Joshua told me. As the chief financial officer for a subsidiary of a business with total revenues in excess of $1 billion, Joshua's social circle did not include any criminals. Yet decisions he had made meant Joshua would soon share all of his meals, his living quarters, and his showers with hundreds of convicted felons for a term of 21 months.

"Can you tell me about yourself," I asked. "Where are you from, what is your educational background, what are your interests?" When advising offenders who contact me, I've found that the more they revealed about their lifestyle and interests, the better I could advise them on steps they could take to make the most of challenging predicaments. I took notes as Joshua opened up.

"I'm 45 years old and I grew up in Chicago," Joshua said. "I come from a family of Jewish faith."

"I'm a member of tribe too," I said. "Were you observant?"

"We attended weekly services and observed the rituals while I was growing up," he told me. "I'm from an orthodox family and we were devout participants in our community. Once I began college I drifted away from the faith, and over time I became more of a secular Jew than one who practiced religion."

"I'm the same, more secular than religious," I said. "Where did you go to school?"

"I went to Northwestern."

"And I presume you studied accounting?"

"That's right. I stayed on to earn an MBA and I graduated in 1990."

"Did you always aspire to pursue a career in business?"

"Well, my father was a lawyer. As a young man I thought about law. But during my undergraduate years I launched a small business installing home sprinkler systems. That sidetracked me. I took a few years off to run the business and I pulled down a decent income. A friend I respected advised that I should return to school and earn my degree. When I did I took up accounting and stuck with it."

"How about after graduation," I inquired. "Did you return to your business?"

"No, by then I wanted to pursue my CPA credentials and to qualify I needed real world experience. I accepted a position with Arthur Andersen, which was one of the "big six" accounting firms. During the first four years of my career I honed my skills by providing auditing and tax services for large corporations."

"Were you aspiring to build a permanent career with Arthur Andersen?"

"I'd say I was open to the possibility, but I was also open to considering other options," Joshua told me. "I worked closely with the CFO's of businesses I was auditing, and when one of them offered me a position as a controller, I accepted."

"What kind of business?"

"It was a large resort, a great job with excellent perks."

"Is that where you stayed?"

"For a few years. I was well compensated and enjoyed the laid back schedule, but I was in my early 40s and ambitious. I could see that another decade would pass before the CFO position opened and I didn't want to wait that long. When another company offered me a CFO position, I accepted."

"And what kind of business was that?"

"We were government contractors, providing hospitality services."

"What size of company was it?"

"The company's overall revenues were $1.2 billion. I was hired with a three-year contract to serve as CFO of a subsidiary of the company, one with $60 million in revenues."

As a government contractor, Joshua explained to me that his company bid to provide services in various parts of the world for the U.S. Government. The contracts required the company to manage food and leisure operations for the military in such remote locations as Guam, Africa, India, even Antarctica. Joshua said that he signed on to lead the subsidiary as CFO, but upon reporting, he was expected to perform as not only the CFO but also assume duties that would ordinarily be assigned to a chief operating officer.

"What type of responsibilities did you have?" I asked.

"As CFO, my duties were to oversee and analyze cash flow, budgeting, accounting operations, and so forth. But the subsidiary was losing money, $2 million a year. In order to ensure its continuity, I would have to take action to turn things around."

"Like what?"

"Like traveling to every location around the world where we had contracts. I'd have to evaluate operations, renegotiate contracts, preside over employment changes that included massive layoffs to bring down labor costs."

"Were you compensated for those additional responsibilities?"

"My contract as CFO provided a salary of $200K, and my bonus would bump it up another $100K. That was decent money, but to earn it I'd have to implement changes that would make the company profitable. In turning the subsidiary profitable, I'd also advance my career."

"So you knew what to expect from accepting the additional responsibilities?"

"Not exactly."

"What do you mean?"

"I didn't fully understand the havoc the job would bring to my personal life."

Joshua was in his early 40s when he accepted the CFO position. He had never been married, but he was in a committed relationship with a woman and he looked forward to starting a family with her. The couple moved in together after he accepted the new job. In accepting the CFO position, Joshua didn't anticipate the tolls of extensive travel. Yet in order to reverse the subsidiary's fortunes, Joshua said that he spent more than three weeks of every month traveling. Within six months, his fiancée moved on. He tried to hold the relationship together, but the separation was too much for her to bear, Joshua said, and he understood her feelings. Breaking his employment contract wasn't a viable option to him because it would have derailed his career. The breakup brought him stress, and as

I listened to Joshua tell me his story, I detected the first prong of the fraud triangle: pressure.

"So how did you respond to the stress that came with the loss of your relationship?" I asked Joshua to continue telling me his story.

"I immersed myself in work," he said. "I've always been a workaholic. With my expanded responsibilities—and no home life to speak of—I lived on continuous company business. Always traveling. Over the next two years I took 120 trips. My life was a whirlwind of hotels and airplanes. The work succeeded in turning the subsidiary profitable, but in the process it ruined my life."

"How so?"

"Well, I've been sentenced to prison. The crime ended up costing me the loss of a $300K income, more than $200K in legal fees, and the humiliation I'm going to live with for the rest of my life."

"I don't want to diminish the anxiety you're going through," I tried to assuage Joshua's worries, "but this setback isn't going to ruin your life. I can help you with some strategies that will put the setback in its proper perspective, possibly even help you emerge from the experience stronger. Before we get into that, tell me what happened. What crime were you convicted of?"

"One count of mail fraud."

"Did you even know what mail fraud was before the government notified you of this offense?" I asked.

"I didn't ever think about it."

I asked Joshua the question of whether he had understood what constituted mail fraud because I knew that most people didn't. When I was a stockbroker I never thought about how my actions could bring charges for white-collar crimes. When I spoke with audiences about ethics, I always tried to show how the federal criminal code related to activities that took place every day, countless times, in every business in America Few people understood that an act as simple as inserting a document in an envelope, sealing it and sending it through the mail could be a federal crime. Of course the criminal code would not apply to people who used the mail for lawful purposes, but if an individual used the mail to send any type of information that furthered a crime, that individual could face criminal charges under Title 18 of the United States criminal code, section 1341, for mail fraud. Such crimes carried a possible penalty of 20 years in prison for each envelope sent.

"What happened in your career that would have exposed you to charges of mail fraud," I asked.

"It's a long story."

"I'm sure it is," I said. "The people I speak to about white-collar crime and the penalties that follow rarely set out to break the law. Circumstances happened. When people made bad decisions, or decisions without considering all of the consequences, criminal charges could follow unexpectedly. What were the circumstances with you?"

"I suppose I began making some questionable decisions when my fiancée and I broke up."

"How so?"

"Every week I visited different cities. The company covered all of my travel expenses, of course, but I saw a loophole that would make my frequent traveling easier to bear. Instead of using my corporate credit card to charge my travel and expenses, I used my personal American Express. The high monthly charges would allow me to accumulate credits like frequent flyer miles and other perks. I could redeem those credits with free airline tickets for women I met who would accompany me on trips. When my bill from American Express came, I simply had the company reimburse me."

"And did the government say that was a crime?"

"That wasn't the crime," Joshua said. "You asked what the circumstances were that led to my charges for mail fraud."

"That's right. Okay. So go on."

"As I saw the privileges accumulating through my AmEx account, I had an idea. Instead of using corporate credit cards to purchase items that furthered company business, I could use my own. My personal credit card didn't have a limit, so I had several duplicate cards delivered to the office. Whenever someone needed to make a purchase for the business, I instructed them to charge the purchase to my personal AmEx."

"Did you have authorization from your colleagues to do business this way?"

"My boss didn't mind at all because the practice lessened reliance on the subsidiary's credit, and when we were working to reverse the business's losses, we welcomed anything that would cut out red tape—like having to extend corporate credit lines."

"Well if you had authorization, I don't see how using your personal credit card for corporate expenses related to mail fraud charges," I said.

"As long as I retained documentation for every purchase and showed how each purchase related to corporate business, there wouldn't have been any criminal charges. But as the months turned into years, I wasn't as scrupulous as I should have been. We charged everything to the credit card, including computers, copiers, even vehicles. My monthly billing statement always showed hundreds of individual charges that when totaled together exceeded $100,000. I didn't want the company to reimburse me directly because passing that much money through my checking account would have raised flags from the IRS. To avoid the complications, I instructed accounting to send corporate checks with my statement directly to American Express to pay the bill."

"And why was that a crime?" I asked.

"The crime was discovered later, after I left the company. My successor saw the massive amounts the company paid to settle my personal credit card statements and suspected fraud. He alerted the U.S. Postal Inspector, and an official investigation began to determine whether I had allowed the business to pay off personal debts as well as corporate debts that were charged to my credit cards."

"Did you?"

"Although not to the extent the prosecutor alleged, I'm embarrassed to admit that I did."

As I listened to Joshua admission, I recognized the second prong of the fraud triangle: capacity. He was the company's chief financial officer. In that position, he had the authority to authorize his colleagues to charge expenses to his personal credit card, and Joshua's accounting staff would not question his instruction to use a corporate credit card bill.

"What prompted you to make such decisions?" I was curious as to what would complete the third prong of the fraud triangle.

"As I said, the slide began with my breakup." Joshua said. "In some ways I blamed the company. When I accepted the job as CFO I didn't expect that it would have such extensive travel demands. But in order to turn the company around I had to accept a more active role in operations and cut costs. I blamed the travel that became necessary for the loss of a valuable personal relationship."

Joshua went on to explain that the initial motivation for charging corporate expenses to his personal credit card was to accumulate frequent flyer miles. He could use those miles to ease his travels by bringing dates with him on trips. The privileges AmEx extended for high monthly charges allowed Joshua to cover the costs for airline tickets and hotel expenses for his dates without having to spend any of his own money.

As the months passed, Joshua's review of corporate expenditures revealed that the travel expenses of his fellow executives far exceeded his own. Those executives charged the company for thousands of dollars in liquor and dining expenses every month; in some cases they even charged for the costs of "travel companions" who accompanied them on corporate trips. Joshua said he authorized payment for those expenses, but since he wasn't a drinker or extravagant diner, he felt that he, too, was entitled to a few perks of the profession.

Since other executives were receiving personal benefits with their excessive expenses, Joshua said that when he submitted his AmEx statement for payment, he began authorizing the accounting department to pay the entire bill—a bill that included both corporate and personal expenses. Rather than reigning in executives for padding their expenditures, Joshua joined them. As Joshua's leadership steered the subsidiary from losses to profitability, it became second nature for Joshua to authorize accounting to pay the entire AmEx bill. He could rationalize the perk as compensation for the duties he performed beyond the scope of the CFO role, for the excessive travel, for his serving the subsidiary as a de facto chief operating officer.

By the time the office of the U.S. Postal Inspector concluded its investigation, the government alleged that of the nearly $2 million that the subsidiary paid to settle Joshua's American Express account, $300,000 of those expenses were personal. As a consequence of Joshua's instructions for the subsidiary's accounting department to send the checks through the mail, the U.S. Attorney's office

Chapter Three

notified him that he was going to face criminal charges for mail fraud.

Notification that Joshua had become the target of a criminal investigation compelled him to hire a defense attorney, and at the defense attorney's urging, a team of investigators who would work to dispute the amount of the fraud. When confronted with the evidence, Joshua acknowledged that he had made some bad decisions with regard to his credit card. The charges humiliated him, bringing high levels of stress, but he maintained that over the three-year period in question, the personal charges did not amount to more than $60,000.

Although Joshua worked closely with the legal team to provide documentation that would prove many of the alleged personal expenses were related to business, too much time had passed and records had been lost. The team could only persuade the government to lower the fraud to $180,000 from $300,000. Since Joshua was a certified public accountant and a CFO, prosecutors said he should have been more diligent about retaining documentation.

"My motivations were never to defraud my employer," Joshua told me. "I know that may not matter much now because the facts speak for themselves. I was pressured in my personal life, stressed and struggling with despondency if not a mild depression. As I think back to what caused all of this, that stress led to some bad decisions that have brought a heavy price for me to pay. Besides preparing to serve a 21-month prison sentence, I've lost my CPA license, disgraced my career, and depleted my savings to pay more than $200,000 in legal fees. And when I walk out of prison, I'll still have $180,000 in restitution to pay."

As the chief financial officer of his subsidiary, Joshua told me that he had the authority to wire transfer as much as $2 million on any given day. With so much access to corporate funds, it seemed clear that Joshua did not have fraudulent intentions when he accepted his position; a fraudulent mind might have misappropriated a much larger sum. Yet Joshua clearly understood "the rules" or the code of his profession. As many white-collar offenders did, he knew right from wrong. Joshua had a fiduciary responsibility to look after the interests of his employer, but imbalances in his personal life and his inattention to ethics prompted Joshua to neglect such duties.

Accepting that he should have known better, Joshua didn't make any excuses for the actions that resulted in his criminal charges. That said, he deeply regretted that he didn't pay more attention to the consequences that could follow any deviation from rightful conduct. It didn't matter that other executives padded expense accounts, as Joshua's legal struggles convinced him that the behavior or practices of others wasn't going to excuse his own conduct. Once government authorities became interested in a case, they would pursue it vigilantly, with an objective of securing convictions and sending a clear message that the government wouldn't tolerate white-collar crime. As Joshua and countless other professionals have learned, defending against such criminal charges could cost an individual everything.

When people like Joshua contacted me for advice to navigate the prison system I was happy to share what I've learned. As I listened to their stories, however, I stood convinced that universities and business organizations could offer real value to society by providing more information on white-collar crime. Too many well-educated people who had positions of leadership made bad decisions without realizing their actions could lead them into the grips of the criminal justice system. Continuing education courses that profiled those who lapsed in their commitment to ethics might persuade more business professionals to make values-based decisions.

Chapter Three Questions

1. How did Joshua's actions differ from his fellow executives who charged excessive expenses to business operations?

2. If Joshua would have required his fellow executives to pay for perks that they had taken for granted, how would his decisions have influenced the morale, or *esprit de corps* in his company?

3. In what ways do executives in other companies make decisions that could expose them to criminal charges?

Chapter Four
Whistle-blowers: The New Corporate Watchdog

In February of 2010, at the invitation of Professor Gia Weisdorn, I addressed an audience at Pepperdine Law School. One guest from the audience asked me about a new whistle-blower initiative by the Securities and Exchange Commission that encouraged people who engaged in fraud or had knowledge of an ongoing fraud to report wrongdoing to authorities. In the past, whistle-blowers laws (codified under Title 18 of the U.S. Code, Section 1514 A) protected employees who reported wrongdoing from retaliation by employers. Under the new initiatives, whistle-blower laws would go far beyond protecting company informants from retaliation. Indeed, even if the whistle-blowers participated in fraudulent activities, new regulations could shield them from prosecution and provide them with economic incentives that included 30 percent of any assets recovered under the fraud.

Those whistle-blower laws were designed to help authorities lower the levels of fraud, deceit, swindles, and wrongdoing. In time, I expected them to bring many more white-collar crimes to the attention of law enforcement. With potential informants all around them, business executives had even more reason to strengthen their ethical cores. Through honest practices, business professionals would keep their good reputations intact; they would also avoid the kinds of cascading personal implosions and humiliations that Eric, one of my clients, expressed after a whistle-blower helped launch an investigation that put everything he held dear in peril.

Eric retained me for consulting services that would help him prepare before he surrendered to federal prison. He had been a senior executive for a health care company, yet some regrettable decisions he made as a corporate leader resulted in his federal indictment, conviction, and three-year prison term. For our first meeting, I agreed to meet Eric for dinner at Katsuya, one of the most popular sushi restaurants in Los Angeles.

I watched as Eric parked his black Mercedes sedan with fancy rims. When he stepped out from the luxury automobile, anyone's first impression of the man would have been that he personified success. He was in his mid-forties, tall with an athletic build, tanned face, and silver hair; he wore a blue suit of the highest quality, crisp white shirt with a gray tie. When we shook hands, he glanced at his watch and apologized for being a few minutes late. The heavy bracelet of his gold Rolex was one more sign of the status symbols he valued, and it suggested that the austerity of imprisonment would not suit him.

After being seated in the trendy restaurant, I asked Eric to tell me more about his life. When he began speaking, he exuded confidence and pride in the considerable accomplishments of his career. In 1996 he earned a business degree at UCLA and then began working for a business that employed more than 100 people. Eric began his career in the accounting department of the company that provided services to the health care industry. After he married, in 1998, he said that aspirations to earn a higher income led him to transition from the accounting department to sales. In 2002 he was promoted to management with the title of vice president of operations.

"Were the prospects of earning a higher income the sole motivation for your switch from accounting to sales?" I wanted Eric to open up about the values that drove him.

"You can't really live in LA without being conscious of status, and I saw limitations in accounting." Eric pulled out his wallet to show me a photograph of his wife. "When Sheila and I married I was auditing the financials. It was all in the numbers. They convinced me that the guys making real money were those on the sales force. If I was going to afford a house on the Westside, I knew I'd have to switch from the fixed salary structure of accounting and move into sales."

"Did the earnings meet your expectations?"

"To an extent. With year-end bonuses I've worked my way to pulling down about three hundo, but it's never really enough. I know it sounds okay, but with taxes taking a big bite, at the end of the day we're left with less than 15 a month. Not easy keeping up in this town on that kind of scratch. What are you going to do?"

I smiled and nodded in empathy, remembering my days as a broker when I was chained up with the same pressures. Since leaving prison I've earned only a fraction of what I used to earn, but my sense of fulfillment exceeds anything I've ever known.

"How is your wife handling these challenges you're facing with the law?" I asked, wanting to know more about his home life.

"Fine." A blank look crossed over Eric's face as if vitality left him.

"Does she comprehend the severity of your prison sentence?"

He shrugged his shoulders, and at once I could see the affected composure vanish. He compressed his lips,

47

brought his closed hand to his chin and lowered his gaze to the table.

"I know this isn't easy," I tried to soothe his nerves, to lift some of the weight that was crushing him. "I've gone through it. In order to help you find your way, I need to know what you're going through, what happened."

Eric shook his head in silence for a moment, then dabbed his eyes with his finger and thumb. "Sheila's left me," he raised his head to look at me, more lines etched into his face, a portrait of sadness, of heartbreak. "She called me a loser, a liar, and said she was going to file for divorce. I can't believe this has happened. Everything I've done has been for her, to give her the house she wanted, the cars, the clothes. I didn't need any of it. I just wanted to please her. But it was never enough. Now she's gone. It's all gone. I can't go to prison," he shook his head. "Three years...I'd rather be dead."

"Don't say such things, Eric. I know it feels like the end, like you've lost everything. But you can pull through this, and I'll help you. Let's start from the beginning. Tell me how you got into this mess. We'll find the way out."

Eric told me that he was charged with numerous crimes related to his indictment in a multi-million-dollar Medicare fraud. At the conclusion of his trial, the jury convicted him of conspiring to defraud the United States by making false statements to Medicare agents both verbally and through letters he sent. The jury also convicted Eric for obstructing a Medicare audit by directing his subordinates falsely to represent that his company was in full compliance with government regulations, and for obstructing a criminal investigation by making false statements to federal agents. A whistle-blower who worked in Eric's company brought the wrongdoing to attention of authorities, and the responses Eric gave to investigators had an escalating influence on the problems he faced.

"I get that a whistle-blower turned you in, Eric. But that doesn't help me understand what it was that you did. Sometimes, to set ourselves back on the right course, we have to begin by reflecting on the decisions we made. At least that was what helped me when I was ready to start putting my life back in order."

Eric nodded. "I had responsibilities as VPO."

"What's that," I asked, "VPO?"

"Vice president of operations. I oversaw several divisions of our company, one of which was testing services for pacemakers."

"Is that the medical device for patients with heart complications?"

"That's right," Eric nodded. "Those devices need regular testing and my company was of the nation's largest test providers."

"How do you test pacemakers?"

"Well I don't do the testing personally." Eric was having a difficult time moving out of denial mode.

"Eric, I understand," I smiled. "I'm not here to prosecute you. The trial's over. I'm just trying to understand why you were charged with federal crimes. It would help if you could explain for me how to test pacemakers."

"We have teams of trained technicians who work in our various facilities," Eric explained. "The technicians use our equipment to test the pacemaker's operation over the telephone lines. Medicare calls it a 30-30-30 test."

"And how does that test work?"

"The technician calls the patient and asks the patient to set up a portable device from home. It transmits signals from the pacemaker that our equipment converts into a conventional ECG report."

"What's an ECG?"

"An electrocardiogram report," Eric continued. "Cardiologists rely on those reports to make sure everything's in order with the pacemaker."

"And was your crime related to those tests that your company performed?"

Eric nodded. "I was found guilty of setting up procedures to shorten the tests, and also for lying about them."

"What would be the motivation for shortening the tests?"

"I'm an operations guy," Eric leaned back in his chair and scratched his scalp. "My job was to increase shareholder value. There were two ways to reach such a goal," he held up one finger, "I could increase revenues," he held up his second finger, "or I could cut costs by running operations more efficiently. Medicare paid a fixed rate for testing each pacemaker, so my job was to increase efficiencies."

"How?"

"Medicare's 30-30-30 test was really three tests that the technician performed," Eric said. "Each test was supposed to last for 30 seconds. The first 30-second test recorded on a magnetic strip the pacemaker's operation in a free running or 'demand mode.' During the first test, the pacemaker supplied an electric charge to the heart only when it sensed that the heart was falling behind the programmed heart rate."

"Okay," I said, following Eric's explanation.

"After that test, the technician recorded on a magnetic strip the pacemaker's operation for 30 seconds in a 'magnetic code', during which the patient would use a magnet to close a switch inside the pacemaker. The magnet caused the pacemaker to send an electric charge to the heart at regular intervals, and the results of the test would reveal for the cardiologist who reviewed the test whether everything was in working order."

"The third 30-second test was when the technician recorded the pacemaker results in the 'demand-after-magnet-mode.' It was a waste of time, really, because it only measured whether the pacemaker returned to free running functioning—but the technician could tell this by listening. Cardiologists only wanted to review results from the first two tests."

"So what happened?"

"The techs had been required to hit a quota of performing four 30-30-30 tests an hour, or 32 tests a shift. But with costs being what they were, and with Medicare refusing to pay more for the tests, the division wasn't really hitting its numbers on 32 tests a day. After considering the data, I didn't see any reason that the technicians couldn't step up their performance to average five tests an hour, or 40 tests per day."

"Would one more test per hour really make that much of a difference?" I asked.

"Not for a single technician, but in the aggregate, when you've got hundreds of technicians performing 40 tests a day instead of 32 tests a day…well, you do the math. The increased quotas would result in 25 percent more revenues without much additional costs to operation."

"Were the technicians able to meet the higher quotas?"

"That became a problem," Eric acknowledged. "To meet the performance quotas, the technicians fudged some on the third test. First they cut it down to 15 seconds, then they stopped running the third test altogether, relying instead on their experience to ensure that they left the pacemaker in its normal functioning mode. Since cardiologists never requested data from the third test," Eric shrugged, "no harm, no foul. There wouldn't have been a

51

problem if one of the technicians who wasn't making the quotas hadn't notified the Department of Health and Human Services."

"Did he report that your company wasn't performing the third test?"

"That's right," Eric said. "One of the managers had fired him after repeated warnings because he wasn't keeping up with the new quotas. To get even, he caused all kinds of problems, and it's pretty much because of him that I'm on my way to prison."

"What happened after the employee notified the government?"

"Well, the first blowup that happened was that the government contractor responsible for disbursing Medicare payments sent a letter to my company announcing that it refused to pay for our pacemaker monitoring because we weren't in compliance with the 30-30-30 test. It was also seeking reimbursement for the Medicare claims it had already paid. The fiasco was going to result in millions of dollars in lost revenues."

"How did you respond to the letter?"

"I immediately drafted a letter to appeal the reimbursement demands and to assert that our company was in complete compliance with all relevant Medicare regulations."

"Wait a minute," I interrupted, "I thought you said that the technicians weren't performing the last test."

Eric held up his hands, palms open, giving me the signal to slow down. "I was overseeing operations, not involved in the minutia of performing thousands of tests. I didn't want to know anything about noncompliance with Medicare."

"But did you know?"

"What I knew was that in order to reach our financial performance objectives we had to increase efficiencies. The managers of each facility oversaw the technicians."

"Did you check with the facility managers before you wrote the letter saying that you were in compliance with all Medicare regulations?"

Eric put down his chopsticks, then scratched his forehead. "You don't know the pressure I was under. When I wrote the letter I was trying to keep the quarterly results from blowing up in my face. Everything was tied to the revenues generated from those tests. If Medicare was going to cease payments and demand reimbursements for the payments it made in the past, well I could see the fallout that would follow. I was just trying to stop the fire before it started burning out of control. I didn't know it was going to keep spreading."

The jury at Eric's trial found him guilty of intentionally making a false statement. When he sent the letters, prosecutors alleged that Eric knew his company was not in compliance with Medicare regulations for the 30-30-30 tests. Jurors unanimously agreed. The United States Code at Title 18, section 1001 makes it illegal for anyone to make false statements to the government.

Whatever the motivations were for Eric to tell the first lie, the problems only grew more severe. After he sent the initial letter in protest of Medicare's refusal to pay for the pacemaker monitoring, the government began to investigate whether Eric's company was in compliance as his letter represented. Investigators spoke with Eric and he verbally told them his company was in compliance. Yet by offering testimony at trial from various facility managers who oversaw the technicians, prosecutors proved to the satisfaction of the jury that Eric was lying when he spoke to investigators. Indeed, the facility managers had testified that they had complained to Eric about the problems that stemmed from the unreasonable quotas he had demanded.

Those lies he told investigators brought additional convictions for Eric, and they led to a government audit.

The United States criminal code under Title 18, section 371, makes "conspiracy to commit offense or to defraud United States" a federal crime. Title 18, section 1516, makes "obstruction of a Federal audit" another federal crime. Both of those statutes carried maximum penalties of five years imprisonment. When Eric sent an e-mail message that instructed the facility managers to tell the government auditors that his company followed the required Medicare procedures (despite his managers having told Eric that in order to meet his quotas the technicians had ceased to perform the final test), he broke both of those laws and the jury convicted him.

Title 18, chapter 47 alone of the U.S. criminal code lists 38 separate categories of federal crimes that fall under the heading "fraud and false statements." Eric did not set out to commit a federal crime—or a series of federal crimes. His only concern, he said, was to increase the financial performance of his company. By improving corporate results, he could justify his bonus, but when he wrote the initial letter, Eric insisted that he was simply trying to protect the company that employed him—not his own compensation. He didn't know that writing a letter could lead to a series of federal criminal charges.

After listening to Eric, I questioned whether mere knowledge of the law would in itself have been sufficient to keep him in compliance. For Eric, the law was nothing more than a book of rules. The deeper problem, I thought, was that Eric's code of values was out of whack. Expecting Eric to have understood thousands of criminal statues, or rules, would have been unreasonable. All he really needed was to understand the importance of making values-based decisions.

Eric's problems did not stem from the letters he wrote or the directions he provided. He may have held the position of corporate leader, but good leadership required an individual to make good decisions, even when confronting challenges. And to make good decisions when confronting challenges leaders must remind themselves what's at stake. Medicare reimbursement policies may have threatened the profit potential in Eric's firm, but the pursuit of profits did not excuse the responsibilities to act with integrity.

Eric was living beyond his means. The decisions he made in his personal life weakened him, making him vulnerable to bad decisions in his professional life. Such pressure caused him to place thoughts about his potential bonus ahead of his duty to lead. That pressure was the root of Eric's problem, not his ignorance of the law. By pressuring his subordinates to circumvent services for which his company was billing, Eric broke numerous laws—despite his denial about "hands on participation." He then made matters worse by lying or dissembling to cover up criminal behavior.

Various fraud and conspiracy statutes were too numerous to count. But in light of their existence, executives in today's environment had all the more reason to cultivate principles of good character. They needed to understand that whistle blower laws made every employee and business partner a law enforcement ally. Someone was always watching, and the government provided meaningful incentives for whistleblowers who reported wrongdoing. Rather than focusing on esoteric laws or rulebooks, executives could avoid the complications that were drowning Eric by following Aristotle's advice on working daily to cultivate character.

Chapter Four Questions

1. How can employers encourage executives to make values-based decisions?

2. How do whistle-blower incentives influence decision making for employees?

3. What differences in culpability exist between the individual who breaks a law from the individual who influenced him to break the law?

Chapter Five
Arthur: A Question of Willful Blindness

In the fall of 2009 I accepted an invitation to speak at DePaul University from Dr. Kelly Pope, professor of accounting. During my imprisonment, I had the privilege of contributing to the education of business students at DePaul. Dr. Pope sent Karen Chodzicki and her team to the prison where I was held in order to video record my descriptions about the pressures and character flaws that led to my downfall. Contributing was a privilege because I found that talking about what happened both cleansed my conscience and opened opportunities to begin a lifelong redemption process that I appreciated. Sometimes people fell of course, and when they did, the spirit of community could help them find their way back. I looked forward to my trip to Chicago so that I could address Dr. Pope's audience in person.

Before I visited DePaul, I participated as a guest on a talk-radio program hosted by Michael Sweig, a law professor at Roosevelt University. Professor Sweig's program discussed business issues, and by interviewing me he exposed his audience to the intricacies of white-collar crime. Then, as I rode in a cab from the radio station to DePaul, I received an email message from Arthur, a listener of Professor Sweig's program. Arthur had listened to the interview and reached out because he was shaken with recent news of his federal indictment. He faced numerous charges for wire fraud.

Remembering a lesson my beloved mother, Tallie, tried to instill in me when I was a child (that in working to help others we simultaneously helped ourselves), and in recognizing the assistance that people like Kelly Pope and Michael Sweig gave me, I acknowledged my duty to help Arthur, even if I could only help by listening. I replied to his email, explaining that I was about to begin my presentation at DePaul, but assuring that I would contact him to listen a few hours later after I finished with the university.

I understood how criminal charges could cripple a person's psyche. Although I would not speak to Arthur for a few hours, I empathized with the mental anguish that was crushing him. I knew it would feel as if the jaws of an iron vise were closing against his head, squeezing the sense of self, the dignity out of him. He was an educated man, a leader, and although I knew that he thought of himself as being good, the indictment shattered that image, obliterating his sense of self. I had struggled through the same anxieties before and knowledge of that pain troubled me as I stepped onto the stage of the auditorium at DePaul.

I didn't know how many times I could speak about my crimes. With every discussion, flashes of humiliation whipped me again. I wondered whether continuing to talk about my complicity in a fraud would keep the wounds open, allowing them to fester rather than heal. In telling my story to the business school students, I saw them sitting attentively in the audience. I responded to their perspective questions and understood their curiosities about the forbidden world of prison. Yet I was sad because I knew that I had once been one of them. I listened to lessons on ethics as a student and as a stockbroker, but back then it would have been easier to imagine myself with leprosy than to imagine myself struggling through problems with the criminal justice system.

My challenge was to help as many people as possible understand that an inattention to ethics could lead anyone astray. I had to convince others of the need to remain attentive to their ethical cores so they could always enjoy the inner peace that came with good character rather than suffer through the turmoil and disgrace that troubled the consciences of Arthur and me.

When I returned to the hotel I met Arthur in a lounge near the lobby. I presumed that he was in his late 60s. Instead of standing straight he stooped and looked as if he had shrunk inside his clothes from the loose way they hung on his long frame. His face was gaunt with crevices in his right cheek and a smoker's rasp. The grip of his handshake felt feeble.

Yet I was wrong about his age. When we sat to talk, Arthur told me that he was a married father of three and only 54. The stress load he was carrying, he said, had aged him. When I asked him to tell me what was going on, he said that everything he had worked for over the course of his life was falling apart because of criminal charges for fraud. They weren't his fault, he insisted, but he didn't know what to do. He didn't think his marriage would survive a prison term, and his children were embarrassed because local newspapers and Internet Web sites had published stories about the accusations against him.

"When you say that you aren't to blame for the charges you face", I asked, "are you saying that crimes weren't committed or that crimes were committed but that you're not guilty?"

"I didn't do anything wrong. My partner deceived me. He's been perpetuating a fraud for more than two years, and now I'm trapped in the middle of it."

"What kind of business were you in?"

Chapter Five

"I'm not in any business now," Arthur said. "The government has shut us down. I was in financial services."

Arthur explained to me that after he graduated from the University of Illinois, he built a career as a commercial real estate broker. He worked with a national brokerage company that specialized in apartment buildings until a few years ago, when he left the firm to form his own business with Mark, an attorney with whom he had worked closely on several deals over the previous decade. Together Mark and Arthur formed a financial services company to take advantage of provisions in the tax code and their respective experiences.

To encourage real estate investment, the Internal Revenue Service offered a section in the tax code to ease some of the income-tax burdens on investors. The IRS certified the provision for real estate exchanged under Title 21 of the United States Code, sections 1030 and 1031. The codes allowed investors who sold commercial real estate investments at a profit to avoid paying capital-gains tax obligations on condition. To avoid paying taxes on the gain, the investors had to use all of the proceeds from the sale of their real estate deal to purchase a new property of equal or higher value. Other conditions required to qualify for the tax break necessitated the seller to purchase new property within 180 days of the original sale, and the seller could not take control of any proceeds from the sale during that interim 180-day period. Accordingly, commercial real estate investors typically entrusted their sales proceeds to a qualified intermediary until they purchased the replacement property that would complete the exchange.

"Over the years of my career in real estate, I built an extensive network of relationships with investors," Arthur told me, "Mark, my partner, had a law practice that specialized in real estate transactions. Since we had a good working relationship, we agreed to form a trust company

60

and facilitate the property exchanges. Mark and I were equal ownership partners in the company," Arthur said, "but we each had specific duties. I was responsible for marketing the services of our firm while Mark had sole responsibility over the legal and financial aspects of the business."

"So how did you market your firm's services?"

"Really, it was all relationship based. When investors I knew sold properties, I spoke with them about opening a trust account with us so our firm could manage the proceeds from the sale of their property until they needed the funds to purchase their new property. If the clients choose to use our services, they would sign standard form agreements providing that property-sale proceeds be wired directly from the closing attorney's account into one of our company's accounts. The clients could choose between a money-market account, yielding a 3 percent return or they could choose an investment account that yielded a 6 percent return."

I stopped Arthur, scratching my head. "I thought these funds had to stay in reserve for the purchase of or exchange of property."

"They were," Arthur answered. "When the clients were ready to close on their next property, our trust would wire the funds. The funds would never pass through the client's hands and thus satisfied the IRS rules."

"I get that the trust may satisfy the IRS for tax purposes—but how could your trust company offer choices of yields such as 3 percent or 6 percent?" I didn't understand how Arthur's company could both hold the proceeds from the real estate sale in reserve—supposedly available on call for the purchase of the exchange property—while simultaneously providing such high rates of return during the interim.

"If the clients chose the money market option," Arthur said, "we would have 48 hours to return the client funds, but if they selected the higher 6 percent yield from the investment account, the client would have to agree to provide 30 days notice for a demand of the money."

"Arthur, you understand that I was a stockbroker before I went to prison?"

"And?" Arthur didn't make the connection to what I was trying to point out.

"In my experience, a close connection exists between risk and return. If you were promising to offer a 6 percent return on an investment, that return would have to come with a certain degree of risk. You understand that investors would consider a 6 percent yield relatively healthy—what kind of investments was your trust company selecting that would kick back investors 6 percent, allowing more for your trust company to profit and still offer the liquidity that would cause your clients to call for their funds within 30 days notice? In all my years as a stockbroker, I never saw such an investment return that wouldn't bring a higher element of risk."

"That's the point," Arthur claimed. "I didn't have anything to do with the funds once they were wired to our company. As far as I knew they were kept in trust. It was my partner, Mark, who was in control of the administration of the business."

"Yet you said you were equal partners in the ownership of the business, right?"

"But my responsibilities were marketing, simply bringing the clients in. Mark had sole authority over the financial business. I assumed he knew what he was doing since he was an attorney."

"Okay. So how did Mark oversee the funds once they were wired to your company's account?"

Arthur explained to me that his partner, Mark, had opened two separate accounts at a major brokerage firm. The first account existed solely as a depository to receive the funds that clients sent upon the closing of their real estate transaction. Once the funds were in hand, Mark transferred them immediately to the second account that he had opened. He used the client funds to trade aggressively in stock options. Over the two years of Arthur's partnership with Mark, Mark's trading of stock options resulted in $11 million in losses for the client funds. For a period of time, Mark succeeded in hiding losses. He sent money that the trust received from new clients to investors who needed their funds to close on their real estate exchange transactions. But in the end, Mark's losses became too large and his scheme collapsed, resulting in criminal charges for 27 counts of wire fraud.

The crime of wire fraud fell under the United States criminal code, Title 18, Section 1343. To convict on charges of wire fraud, the government had to prove that a defendant intended to use communication lines to defraud others. The crime of wire fraud exposed people to sentences of up to 20 years for each conviction. In facing 27 counts, theoretically Arthur could spend the rest of his life in prison.

"But I didn't do anything wrong," Arthur insisted. "Our partnership agreement clearly identified my responsibilities as marketing. Mark was in charge of all administrative responsibilities, including setting up the accounts and presiding over all financial transactions. I'm not the one who lost the clients' money."

Whether the government would prove that Arthur was complicit in fraud was a legal matter, one that a competent defense attorney would have to help him resolve. As I sat listening to him in that hotel lobby, I explained that I couldn't have any role in offering advice on legal matters. Yet through my work, I explained, I learned of a concept that existed in criminal law called "willful blindness." Under the theory of willful blindness, courts could deem statements or representations fraudulent if they were made in a conscious indifference to the truth.

Arthur had a long and costly legal battle ahead of him, one for which he was not prepared. An unfortunate reality of my work put me into conflict with many people who were at the lowest moments of their lives. They stood to lose their families, their assets, their reputations, their careers, and their liberty. Some contemplated suicide. As I reflected on Arthur's repeated insistence that he hadn't done anything wrong, my mind wandered back to those business school students I had addressed only hours before at DePaul. How many of them would venture into careers with the misunderstanding that they could protect themselves from legal complications with simple claims of ignorance of the wrongdoing around them?

Arthur may cling to his claims that he limited his responsibility to marketing but I wondered how plausible such claims would be in light of his ownership interest in the trust company. He had graduated from college and had built a long career related to investments. Such experience might suggest that he bore some legal responsibility for understanding how his company intended to deliver the yields his marketing efforts promised clients while the trust company simultaneously promised liquidity. Arthur may claim that he didn't know anything about the inherent risk of trading stock options and the inconsistency of his partner's using clients' funds for such trades while promising security, but those claims would not excuse him from exposure to decades in prison if he were convicted on 27 counts of wire fraud that resulted in $11 million in losses.

It saddened me to know that the only service I could offer Arthur was to listen. Nothing I said was going to reverse the reality that he had offered a service to investors that, in the end, turned out to be a Ponzi scheme. His partner may have acted alone in squandering client funds through imprudent market speculations but Arthur had presented those investors with documents offering an unreasonably high rate of return on funds that were supposed to be held in trust. He should have known more about how his company was going to provide such yields—especially since he was a principal of the trust company.

My experience might help Arthur prepare for the adversity awaiting him. But my real challenge was to offer suggestions to prevent others from making decisions that could lead them into similar difficulties. Arthur was but one of millions of people who convinced themselves that they were merely businessmen or someone who delivered a product or service. I hoped to reach more before bad decisions derailed their lives. The truth was—as I had learned—when we made representations that others relied upon, we had an ethical responsibility to act honestly and with integrity—regardless of our legal obligations. Acting honestly and with integrity would not only ensure that we avoided troubles with the criminal justice system, such behavior would keep us on track for happiness and inner peace.

As my brother Todd and I were growing up, Tallie admonished us to make all decisions as if someone we loved and respected was watching us. Could we feel proud of the choices we made and defend them? Had I used my mother's guidance for all of my decisions I would not have become enmeshed in the kinds of deceitful behavior that later led to my imprisonment. It took significant strength for me to see the wisdom and long-term benefit of making values-based decisions. As I listened to Arthur, he sounded lost in those same clouds of denial that once blinded me.

From the writings of Professor Jana Craft, I developed a series of questions that I would rely upon to guide me like a compass through the quagmires of life. I wrote about them in my book, *Lessons from Prison*:

1) Would my decisions mislead anyone or obscure truth?

2) Could I justify my decisions to my unborn child whom I would want to consider me as a man of honor?

3) Would others judge my motivations and actions as being consistent with the concepts of integrity and good citizenship?

Those were not the questions that guided my decisions or my conscience once I became a stockbroker. As a consequence I lost my way through detours I misperceived as shortcuts, and they resulted in my becoming disgraced with the label of a convicted felon. It may have been too late to steer Arthur away from legal troubles similar to those that had cost me so much. His insistence that he did not know about his partner's misappropriation of client funds might suspend some of the pain as he proceeded through the judicial system. But a grand jury and a prosecutor wanted to hold Arthur accountable for $11 million of client funds.

We all could learn from the troubles Arthur faced. Regardless of his legal outcome, as a person others trusted and relied upon, he had an ethical duty to represent his clients fairly. Had Arthur prefaced his representations with a question like, "Would my actions mislead anyone or obscure truth?" perhaps he would not have been struggling through the anxieties that so paralyzed him when we met in that hotel lobby.

Chapter Five Questions

1. What role does trust have in careers of sales executives?

2. How should executives balance allegiances to company with allegiances with clients?

3. Compare and contrast duties to legal and ethical codes.

Chapter Six
Steve's Tax Scam

My past experiences of growing up as a privileged Jewish kid from Encino, and going on to play baseball at USC before beginning a lucrative career as a stockbroker may make it easy for university students and business executives to identify with me. The part of my personal story that distinguishes me from others was the diversion I took through the criminal justice system, the lessons I learned from prison, and the perspective that I have lived with since my mother drove me home from the prison camp in Taft, California. I've come to call that perspective ethics in motion.

The perspective implies a more comprehensive understanding of my role in society. When I was a stockbroker I once joked that I would manage anyone's money—including money that belonged to anti-Semitic groups. As events turned out, I had to accept that my warped sense of values led to business and personal decisions that became worse and worse. The consequences they brought convinced me of the need to change. In my case, I knew that change would require daily introspections—self-questioning about whether my motivations and actions were consistent with the values of honesty and integrity that I identified as driving me.

A few months after I established my consulting business that would specialize in guiding white-collar offenders who faced their own struggles with the criminal justice system, I received a call from Steve. That call would test my resolve. I had to pay bills and I was struggling through the cash flow problems that afflicted many small business owners. Steve's call brought an opportunity to earn a few thousand dollars at a time when I could have really used the income.

Steve told me that he was being indicted for tax fraud and that he was facing up to 20 years in prison. I made it clear to Steve that I was not an attorney. My area of expertise, I explained, was limited to sharing what I had learned through my prison experience. By doing so I would work to help others discover strategies to emerge stronger through their own challenges. Steve said he was working with counsel to persuade the government to reduce his exposure and that he wanted me to describe what he might expect. I told him my fee and Steve remitted payment through my Web site at once. The consultation began through our Web conference.

"Tell me about the charges you're facing." I inquired about the problems that led him to me.

"Prosecutors are alleging that I set up a tax scheme that resulted in the loss of $39 million worth of tax collections. It's a preposterous allegation."

"And how did prosecutors identify you as a target for the criminal prosecution?"

"A no-good snitch who was out to save his own behind," Steve was still angry. "Guy was caught running a Ponzi scheme and sentenced to serve a few years for ripping off his investors. To reduce his sentence, he cut a deal with the feds. I was the bait."

"Steve, as we begin it's important to me that you understand my role. I'm here to listen, but ultimately my goal is to give you a perspective that might help you reach the best possible outcome going forward."

"Yeah man, I got you, I get it."

"To reach that goal," I continued, "we're going to need some balance. We need to analyze all options objectively, and that requires us to suspend judgments as we evaluate how we can make the best overall decisions. My approach has taught me that anger, or blaming others for problems doesn't help."

"I'm with you," Steve said. "I just get a little worked up when I think about it."

"Good. Now help me understand why the informant would have given your name to the prosecutors."

"I told you. He was guilty of running a Ponzi scheme. The only way he could reduce his sanction was to help prosecutors indict someone else."

"But why did the informant give prosecutors your name? What did the informant say that you did?" I was careful with my words so as not to make a judgment call as to Steve's guilt or innocence.

"I'm a CPA in Fort Lauderdale. My practice specializes in tax matters for high net-worth individuals. Besides preparing tax forms for clients, I also put investment syndications together for them and I served as the general partner. The informant was a partner with me in a real estate project one of my syndications operated. As a partner, he was privy to the scheme."

"Am I to understand you to say that there was a scheme?"

"Of course there was a scheme! What do you think we are talking about here, Sunday school? It just wasn't a $39 million scheme."

"So you're not going to contest your guilt of participating in a tax fraud?" I needed some clarity.

"You're planning to cooperate with the government and to plead guilty, is that right?"

"That depends on whether my attorney can bring the prosecutors down from the $39 million."

"I see. So it's the amount of tax fraud that's in dispute, not whether you engaged in fraud."

"That's right."

"And how do you feel about admitting to being involved in a fraud?"

"What do you mean?"

"Well, have you given any thought to the victims from the fraud?" I was trying to gauge whether Steve felt any remorse for his criminal actions.

"Victims?" Steve was taken aback by my question. "What are you talking about? I'm the only victim here! I couldn't care less about any victims! Besides, the government is hardly a victim. Don't you know the government is the biggest crook of all? Every time one of those politicians passes a bill, don't think for a second that he's not lining his own pockets with some kind of perk."

"But how does wrongdoing by someone else excuse our own actions?" I was trying to nudge Steve, gently, into recognizing and accepting responsibility, or at least to consider it, so we could create a strategy that would begin reconciliation. "Shouldn't we at least strive to live honestly?"

"Look pal, I don't know where you've worked. In my town, if an accountant is going to be worth his salt, he's got to be willing to push the envelope. That's it. He can't get all sentimental about the nonsense. How else is he going to survive? If I couldn't cut or eliminate tax bills, what's to distinguish me from the next guy?"

I continued to try bringing Steve around, but after 30 minutes of conversation, I told him that I was going to refund his money. That was a big step for me because the money was in my account already and I really needed it. If I were to accept the money, I would be living contrary to the values of honesty and integrity that I committed to living every day. I didn't want that kind of contradiction or disharmony.

"What do you mean you're refunding my money?" Steve was incredulous.

"I just don't think we're going to be able to work together," I said. "I can't help you."

"Look I know you might not be able to get me out of this," Steve wanted to continue. "But I need some advice on how to get through it. I'm facing 20 years man, and I'm paying you big money. I got a right to tell it like it is."

Steve was looking for someone who would feed into his I'm-a-victim mentality, and some kind of artifice that might lessen his liability. "I'm sorry," I said. "The services I offer differ from my competitors. I wish you the best, but I'm going to have to pass." I refunded the retainer in full.

When I was a stockbroker, I would have more readily agreed to part with a limb than to return a client's money. I wouldn't have cared what would I would have had to say, but the money was staying with the firm. Despite the corporate codes, my brokerage firm paid me to build account balances—not to return funds because I was troubled with pangs of conscience.

As a consultant, deceit would have been much easier. I knew that Steve was in a vulnerable state and I knew what he wanted to hear. He eagerly wanted to pay someone who would agree that fraud was acceptable, and he sought guidance on how to perpetuate the fraud with tricks that might somehow give him an edge or lower his exposure to sanctions. Yet with the commitment I had made to ethics, I couldn't permit myself to become part of anything that wasn't consistent with good values.

Somehow, my response to Steve's refusal to act responsibly strengthened me inside even if it weakened my bank account.

When I spoke in corporate training seminars, I suggested that businesses could advance their long-term interests by rewarding executives who acted in accordance with good ethics. My experience in the corporate environment was that businesses rewarded executives for closing deals, but not always for doing the right thing. If an executive came across a deal that failed to pass the ethical test, then the executive shouldn't have any dilemma about turning it down. Employers should encourage and applaud such leadership, and they should recognize the enterprise value of honesty in a meaningful way.

When executives perceived such appreciation from their profession, more would refrain from ethical misconduct that could expose the individual and the corporation to severe sanctions for white-collar crimes. Sometimes that commitment to honesty would yield even more value down the line, as I surprisingly discovered when Steve called me back a few days later after I had returned his money.

"I know I said some things that I shouldn't have the last time we spoke," Steve told me. "I'm under a lot of stress right now, as this is the first time I've faced criminal charges. But after speaking with a few others who offered to help, I realized that I liked your approach best and I'd appreciate it if you would work with me to get through these problems."

"The thing about it," I told Steve, "is that my approach centers on the need to accept responsibility. That means finding or creating steps we can take to demonstrate that we know we've done something wrong, taking actions that show we want to reconcile with society for the bad decisions we've made, and showing our commitment to righting our values so we can live as honorable, contributing members of society. Self preservation must be subordinate to responsibility, not the other way around."

"I can't make promises," Steve said. "But I'm willing to listen and to learn."

"And I appreciate your sincerity, but I won't take anyone's money if I don't think I can help. To help you I would I need to understand more about the motivations that led to tax fraud and to believe that you would join me in finding solutions that might demonstrate your remorse. That was the strategy I used to turn my life around, and it's the one I believe in. If you think that's what you're after, we can work together, otherwise I can't help you."

"Let's move forward," Steve agreed.

"Okay. Tell me what happened, what you did—not about the informant snitching on you, but what you're responsible for."

"I told you that my accounting practice specialized on taxation services for wealthy individuals. My clients frequently invested in syndications I put together that delivered healthy income streams. Those syndications usually offered investors a great return, but the real value I provided was in structuring deals that offered depreciating benefits that could offset their income. On occasion, as economies turned unexpectedly, a deal didn't work out as expected. Anyone could boast that every deal was a winner, but a loser did surface every now and again. That's just the way business worked out."

"Was it a loser that brought you these problems," I asked.

"Not the deal so much as the way I converted an investment that was losing money into a net winner for the participating investors."

"And how did you do that."

"By checking a box basically," Steve was proud of the creative thinking it took to come up with the tax ruse.

"The investment had turned, with depreciation resulting in millions of dollars of annual losses. I was the general partner, and all the investors in the syndication were clients of my accounting practice. They were big earners, each with W-2 forms showing several million dollars worth of annual income. As passive investors they weren't entitled to write off the operating cost of the syndication. To help them lower their income-tax obligations I created the appearance that passive investors were actually active in the business. That ruse permitted them to offset losses against their income, substantially decreasing each investor's annual tax bill."

"So you knew what you were doing was illegal?"

"Of course."

"Why would you knowingly commit a crime and expose yourself to possible criminal sanctions if the benefits would only flow to wealthy investors?"

"Those investors were my clients and I had an obligation to serve them to the best of my ability."

"That obligation didn't include fraud," I pointed out. "You put them into a legitimate investment that didn't turn out well. Those investors were big boys, with millions in annual income. Presumably, they understood the risk. Why did you have to break the law?"

"Look," Steve wanted to explain himself. "I liked the challenge of figuring out solutions to complex problems. That's what I do; it's the reasons my clients pay me. If one of my partners hadn't been indicted for running a Ponzi scheme, then dropped the dime on me, no one would have known."

"Have you thought at all about the victims that resulted in your participation in a fraud?"

Chapter Six

"Who's the victim?" Steve didn't see any wrong in the felony he committed. "Are you telling me that I'm supposed to consider the government a victim? The IRS? That's ridiculous."

"How about your wife, your children?" I asked. "Have you thought about how being indicted for fraud might influence their lives? One of the lessons I learned from my experience with the criminal justice system was that I wasn't alone. I was part of a community. When I was perpetuating lies as a stockbroker, I didn't consider anything but my income, my desires. Yet after my troubles with the law began, I saw the pain and humiliation my crimes brought to the people I loved. My mother had to begin therapy with a psychologist to work through the pain I caused. What would a conviction for fraud and a long prison sentence do those who love you? Have you thought about that?"

Steve paused. "My wife wouldn't be able to handle the disgrace."

"How about all of the employees who work for your firm? How about all the people who trust you, and your obligations to your profession? And what about your clients? How will they feel about government investigators inquiring about their business affairs or finances because your ingenious fraud that supposedly no one could discover brought them to the attention of IRS agents?"

Steve looked at me through the Web camera but he was silent, as if all the ancillary consequences that accompany criminal problems were suddenly becoming clear to him, like an unexpected punch to the nose.

"You may not feel morally impugned for using your intelligence to cheat the government out of tax revenues, but what about your reputation?" Another lesson I learned from my experience was that in breaking the law, I dealt a real blow to my sense of good character.

76

"I hadn't thought about the problems in those terms," Steve was speaking with less energy, as if he had been deflated.

"That's understandable," I said. "Instead of seeing the problems we create with clarity, we seem to have a default mechanism of denial. I know I did. Denial numbs us from the pain and can blind us into even accepting that we've done anything wrong. More than three years passed before I came to terms with all the damage I had caused through my participation in deceit, and it's going to take me a lifetime to make things right. I'm still working every day to redeem myself. But I've got to tell you, a liberty and a sense of cleansing comes once we begin working to set things right."

"I wouldn't even know where to begin."

"To begin," I told Steve, "you have to acknowledge that you're part of a larger community than yourself. As members of that community, we all have a duty to live honestly, to act fairly, transparently. If prosecutors are threatening to charge you with a $39-million dollar fraud, and you're contesting the amount of the fraud—as opposed to whether a fraud was committed—perhaps we ought to begin by working to restore some of your credibility."

Steve came on board. While his attorney continued negotiations with prosecutors, Steve took an active role by volunteering as a mentor in a local community center for at-risk kids. In working closely with teens who came from disadvantaged backgrounds, Steve said that he began to appreciate the responsibility that accompanied his privileged position in society.

"These kids have had a rough start," Steve observed. "With the struggles of their parents, and their lack of positive role models, it's no surprise they're in trouble. I don't have an excuse." His change in perspective led to a more hands-on approach to resolving his problem with the government.

After several more months of negotiations, Steve's defense attorney had convinced prosecutors to reduce Steve's culpability from a $39 million fraud to a $21 million fraud, but the government was still inclined to indict him on charges that could bring a nine-year sentence. In an effort to clarify his actions I worked with Steve to draft a narrative—from start to finish—that described his role in orchestrating the tax ruse. He included a detailed spread sheet that identified the tax obligations of each individual involved, explained his motivations for putting the scheme together, and described why he came to regret his actions. Steve used the report to persuade those investors who benefited to settle with the government. Instead of a $39 million loss, or a $21 million loss, Steve showed that the total loss to the government was $9 million in uncollected income tax. Of the 11 investors who had participated, 10 agreed to make things right by paying all back taxes, penalties and interest while amending their previous tax returns; Steve accepted full responsibility for creating the tax scheme, but through the narrative and with the amended tax returns, he showed that the total loss to the government was less than $1 million in uncollected income tax.

The documentation Steve provided, along with his success in persuading his clients to settle their tax obligations, his acceptance of responsibility, and the extensive efforts he made to contribute to society while working through the investigation made the prosecutor more inclined to show Steve leniency. Rather than indicting him for a fraud that would have exposed Steve to 20 years in prison, the government entered into a plea agreement with him. The agreement permitted Steve to plead guilty to a single count under Title 26 of the US code, Section 7201, for the crime of "Attempt to evade or defeat tax," which exposed him to a maximum sanction of five years imprisonment.

Before setting myself on this new course of ethics in motion, I would not have invested the energy to work with Steve to the extent that I did. Instead I would have accepted his payment and told him exactly what he wanted to hear—that the problems weren't his fault and that the informant was to blame for all of Steve's problems.

I will not allow those deceptions to poison my life or business practices again, as I have found life much more rewarding when I rely upon honesty and integrity as my guides. Steve has made the same change, as he introduced me to his attorney and colleagues, telling them that I've influenced his perspective on life. Those recommendations from Steve brought opportunities to expand my speaking and consulting business, further convincing me that doing what is morally required is not always unprofitable.

Chapter Six Questions

1. Describe how community service can influence values.

2. Why would Steve observe that as a professional he had a higher level of culpability that his clients who benefited from the scheme?

3. How does lack of a perceptible victim influence the possibility for white-collar crime?

Chapter Seven
Dr. Gary's Seven Patient Files

In the fall of 2009 I participated in a radio interview with Frank Mottek on KNX 1070 in Los Angeles. Frank's business program is popular, with more than 50,000 listeners every day. He invited me to speak with him and his listeners about ethics, morality, and the consequences that followed when we crossed the line. Not everyone agreed that I was worthy of such a forum.

Indeed, within a few days of my radio interview with Frank I received my first piece of hate mail. The letter, in summary, clarified the writer's view that felons forfeited the right to speak about ethics or morality. He berated me as scum, expressed hope that others had abused me in prison, and wrote that as a convicted criminal, I should recognize that I'm an outcast in society and that I should act accordingly by remaining in the outskirts.

Receiving the letter was sobering. It reminded me that regardless of my efforts to reconcile with society and to atone for the bad decisions I made as a stockbroker, some would never accept that I had any value to offer. Reading such hateful words made me feel alone. In my mind, they put me right back in prison, where correctional counselors would speak condescendingly to me, or ask questions such as whether this was my first crime or simply the first time I was caught.

Chapter Seven

If I were to hide from the bad decisions of my past I might lessen my exposure to such slaps in the face. Hiding from my past, however, would be more like wearing a band aid that simply covered up my character flaws, and I wanted to redeem them. Others who've never been convicted of a felony would think of themselves as being better people then I was, and maybe they were right. But in telling my story I was convinced that I could help others embrace the practical reasons for acting ethically at all times.

Media reports made clear that a need existed to show others that simple slips in ethics could lead to cascading problems—including felony convictions and the lifelong ramifications that accompanied them. A single day did not pass in our society when news sources wouldn't publish a story about some pillar of society who made a bad decision that exposed him to the unforgiving wrath of the criminal justice system. Those stories described the fall of people who considered themselves ethical, good citizens. As I listened to or read those news reports, I realized how easily anyone who didn't make a daily commitment to cultivating a strong ethical core could begin a series of decisions that might bring irreversible consequences.

Even political leaders who promoted themselves as ethical purists were vulnerable to making decisions that could derail their lives. For example, John Ensign was a United States Senator from Nevada who promoted himself as a champion of family values. Yet *The New York Times* published a huge story revealing that while Senator Ensign was pontificating about the importance of ethics, he was betraying his wife, family, and close friend by carrying on an affair with his close friend's wife. To make matters worse, Senator Ensign—a lawmaker—conspired to cover-up the affair by paying off his "friend" with cash and a lobbying job with a Nevada company that would benefit from close access to Senator Ensign. The story not only published a sizzling example of Washington hypocrisy, but also illustrated a need in society to show the consequences that could follow a lapse in ethics.

This need has existed since the beginning of recorded history. The New Testament told us that when he was urged to condemn a woman for immoral conduct, Jesus responded by suggesting that he who was without any character flaws should cast the first stone. None of the accusers were without flaws, and all walked away. Although my background may have been from the Jewish faith, I understood Jesus' message. Despite everyone's capacity to make bad decisions, some people in society would be inclined to ignore their own character flaws and potential for downfall.

Since I was living through the consequences, I was more inclined to empathize when others described their troubles. The more examples I heard from people who once thrived as community leaders, the more I hoped that in sharing what I had learned I could help others avoid their own downfall.

Besides exposing me to the listener who castigated me with hate mail, my radio interview on Frank Mottek's program introduced me to Gary, a community leader whom I wish that I could have reached before his own tragic downfall. Unfortunately, my message did not reach Gary until he had gone through his own troubles with the judicial system. After hearing my interview, Gary called me for advice that might help him through the 57-month prison term he was about to begin serving.

Following our television conversation, we agreed to meet for a longer discussion and I drove to Gary's home in a gated community. I met his wife, Karen, and the couple's 10-year-old son, Brandon. The modern home overlooked a private tennis court and pool that was surrounded by manicured lawns; tall shrubbery provided privacy. Gary was a physician, and his home suggested that he led a successful, lucrative practice. We spoke about his background.

Gary grew up in Seattle, one of three boys. His parents were well-educated professionals who had emigrated to the U.S. from Vietnam. "My father was always studying and he impressed upon my brothers and me the importance of education," Gary said. "He had been from a wealthy Vietnamese family, but in coming to the U.S. he had left everything behind and started from scratch. My father always said that education was the best investment anyone could make because no one could ever take away what was in the mind. He earned a Ph.D. and built a successful career designing billing systems for hospitals."

"Was it your father who persuaded you to pursue a career in medicine?" I asked.

"He didn't suggest medicine," Gary shrugged. "We were a very close family and he wanted my brothers and me to study hard but to pursue careers that interested us. I respected my father, and through him I learned to love studying. I still do. But even though I was a straight-A student, I didn't think I would grow to become a doctor. My girlfriend from high school planned on studying medicine and she convinced me that since I liked people so much I should do the same."

Gary studied biology and chemistry at the University of Washington, graduating in 1987, then continued through medical school, earning his MD in 1991. From Washington he went to Stanford for a three-year internship, and in 1994 Gary began his career in internal medicine. When we spoke, in the spring of 2010, he was 46 and had been practicing for 16 years.

For the first 12 years of his career, Gary worked primarily in geriatric care. He liked older people, he said, and for three years he served as the CEO of a group of long-term, acute care specialists with combined annual revenues in excess of $120 million. When Gary accepted the position the hospital chain was losing money; an administrator with a background in business rather than medicine was running the hospital. As a physician, Gary was more effective as an administrator. His medical knowledge gave him an advantage in negotiating contracts with insurance companies and in selecting which patients to accept. Through management efficiencies that Gary initiated, he steered the company from seven-figure annual losses to annual profits that surpassed $8 million. Such success led to the chain becoming an acquisition target by a publicly traded health care provider. Gary resigned after the corporate sale and began his own practice as an internist in 2006.

In addition to building a successful career in medicine, Gary was active with Karen in strengthening their community. "Both of our families were from Vietnam, and we've been blessed with extraordinary privilege. We have a responsibility, and because of it we enjoyed working together to contribute our time and resources."

Gary and his wife were active in organizing groups of physicians who would join them in donating their time to provide medical care to the needy both in the United States and abroad. Each year he and his wife would spend two weeks in Vietnam, and while there he would work in rural communities with village leaders to improve health care services. Besides donating his medical expertise, Gary was active with his Christian faith and he volunteered 10 hours every week to teach Catholicism.

Gary's reputation as a role model and ideal citizen made him an unlikely candidate for the criminal justice system. At his sentencing hearing, the bishop from his church and other leaders spoke as character witnesses for him, testifying about the selfless contributions Gary and his family made to strengthen the community. Nevertheless, the judge imposed a 57-month sentence on Gary. As we spoke he expressed sorrow about the imminent separation from his family, but he refused to make any excuses.

"Well, tell me how a man like you even becomes the target of a criminal investigation." As I sat across from him on a leather chair beside a large aquarium filled with tropical fish, I found it hard to believe that he would soon self-surrender to federal prison.

"One of my patients was arrested," Gary explained. "She had been suffering from endometriosis, a condition that can cause abnormal bleeding and severe pain. To treat her condition I used a prescription for Vicodin, which the DEA classified as a Schedule II narcotic. Police arrested her when they caught her attempting to sell the drugs on the street."

"But what does one of your patients selling drugs illegally on the street have to do with you prescribing Vicodin as a pain medication?"

"The DEA's investigation revealed that the patient had obtained the Vicodin she was selling from a prescription that I wrote. That was all it took for the DEA to begin investigating me."

"Wait a minute." The explanation didn't make sense to me. I scratched my head, as I always do when I don't understand something. "You're a medical doctor. You diagnosed a patient with a medical problem. You prescribed the patient medication that was appropriate for her condition. Then she resold the prescription. You're telling me that scenario was sufficient to launch a criminal investigation?"

"Whenever I wrote a prescription I was required to write it in triplicate," the doctor explained. "One copy stayed in my file. One copy was for the patient. The third copy went to the pharmacy. When the pharmacy received the prescription, it entered it into the CURES system."

"What's the CURES system?"

"It's a national database that tracks what medication a patient was receiving," Gary explained. "It was designed to track doctors and patients and the prescriptions of medications. That way, if a patient was visiting multiple doctors to receive additional medications, the CURES system could alert the doctor. I don't know what my patient told the DEA agents. She was selling the Vicodin with a group of others. Through the database system, the DEA could track that I wrote the prescription for the Vicodin she was selling. With that information, the DEA concluded somehow that I was involved and they obtained search warrants for my home and office."

The story was unbelievable to me. I looked around Gary's exquisite home. It was tastefully decorated with original artwork hanging on the walls, expensive furniture, high-end electronics and appliances. "Out of curiosity, Gary, what's your annual income range?"

"I earn anywhere between three-hundred to six-hundred thousand dollars per year."

"And with that level of income, the DEA agents suspected you of being involved in a street-level drug conspiracy?"

"I don't know what they suspected. All I can tell you is that the team of agents charged in here with guns drawn. They handcuffed my wife and me, ordering us not to move from this couch while they searched the house. When they didn't find anything of value, they drove me to my office and they confiscated 1,200 of my patient files, my record books and computer system. They didn't arrest me, but they gave me a summons that ordered me to report for a court hearing the following day. I was charged with conspiracy to distribute drugs."

"How did your wife respond to all of that drama, with federal agents searching inside your beautiful home and ransacking through your belongings?"

"How do you think?" Gary shrugged, opened his hands. "She felt violated, we both felt violated. Thank God Brandon was in school so he didn't have to see it."

"What happened next?"

Gary explained that after he reported as directed to the federal courthouse the following day, a judge allowed him to return home provided that he complied with all scheduled judicial requirements. Gary retained a defense attorney. "The first order of business," he said, "was meeting the attorney's demand for a $100,000 retainer that he would bill against at $500 per hour. I understood those were only the beginnings of my expenses and that this matter could become very costly."

As the government continued its investigation, federal officers examined all 1,200 patient files that they had confiscated from Gary's office. The search revealed that Gary prescribed Vicodin appropriately to the woman with endometriosis; her file was in order and in compliance with the law. In going through the 1,200 files, however, the agents discovered seven separate files that were not in order.

"What was wrong with them?" I asked.

"As a medical doctor, I was licensed to prescribe medication. But every prescription required strict documentation. To be in compliance with the law, every patient file had to identify the patient's subjective complaint, the doctor's objective observations, the doctor's assessment, and the plan of action. We used an acronym called SOAP, which stood for Subjective, Objective,

Assessment, and Plan. In the seven files that led to my problem, I didn't sufficiently document the files to meet the threshold of legal compliance."

"Like what," I asked. "What didn't you document?"

Gary explained to me that the seven files recorded his assessments and treatment of long-term patients whom he knew well. He understood their conditions. Rather than writing out the details, Gary used a shorthand symbol that indicated no change in conditions with each of the SOAP inquiries.

"And that wasn't sufficient?" To me, Gary was describing a clerical error, not a federal crime that would warrant a 57-month prison term.

"It wasn't sufficient because although I was familiar with the patient's health status, and I understood what I meant by the no change symbol, if another doctor were to consult the patient's file that symbol would not provide the necessary information for the doctor to treat the patient."

Gary went on to explain what happened with the seven files. He regularly treated 50 patients on any given day at his office. That busy scheduled necessitated his writing with shorthand in the files during the consultation. In the evening, when the practice quieted down, Gary would complete the paperwork of the files by elaborating on each patient's condition. But the seven files in question recorded visits from patients on an afternoon two years before the files were seized by the DEA. Gary's journal showed that he had left on his annual trip to Vietnam the day after those seven patients had visited. He was likely rushing, and in his haste, he said that he must have set the files aside—without completing them. His clerical assistant must have then returned the patient files to their place of storage without Gary's update.

By not updating those patient files, the prescriptions for medicine that Gary made in those seven instances were

89

in violation of Title 21 of the United States criminal code, section 841, which made it illegal for anyone to distribute a controlled substance except as authorized by law. Prosecutors told his attorney that the government was prepared to charge Gary with 15 counts of writing prescriptions without appropriate documentation. Those crimes would result in a possible sentencing range of between 70 and 87 months.

"So did you make a plea agreement?"

"I had to," Gary took a sip from a glass of iced tea. "My attorney told me that the jury would have convicted me during a trial because there wasn't any way we could defend against the charges. The prosecutors had the seven files in evidence, and they clearly showed that I had written the symbol for no change rather than the appropriate documentation. He couldn't defend against what I didn't write, so he negotiated a sentence of 57 months in exchange for my guilty plea.

Negotiating that plea agreement, Gary said, took three years and cost more than $160,000 in legal fees. His life was a roller coaster during that time because he had no resolution. There was always waiting and the waiting brought more stress. He lost his license to practice medicine, at least for the time being, and that hurt because his identity was closely aligned with his profession. I empathized with Gary as I suggested strategies he could embrace through imprisonment that would assuage some of the pain that would come with his separation from family and community.

When I asked Gary whether his conviction had any moral or ethical implications, he nodded sadly and spoke of his regrets.

"I was a medical professional and I had responsibilities to all of my patients. I could cite excuses all day long about how busy I was, but over these past three years I've had to accept that I should have been more careful with my charting. Those charts needed to be current at all times in case another doctor ever had to evaluate the patient. Keeping those files current was my duty as a doctor and it was the law. I regret that I neglected my duty with those seven files. I can't blame anyone but myself. Ethics required a duty to my responsibilities, and with those seven files I regret that I had failed. Whatever time pressures I was under, I shouldn't have neglected my responsibility to those patients or my profession."

When Gary spoke with such humility about his responsibilities to his profession, I thought about how admirably he was in accepting his own fate. In a way, Gary reminded me of the story of Socrates, who agreed to self-induce his poisoning as a consequence of a judicial system's ruling in ancient Greece. On the other hand, Gary's response differed remarkably, I thought, from Senator Ensign, who didn't consider his responsibility to act ethically as a U.S. senator quite the same way.

Chapter Seven Questions

1. How can neglecting duties to your profession lead to criminal prosecution?

2. What steps are available for professionals who want to redeem ethical violations?

3. How will Gary's breach of responsibility with regard to those seven files influence the rest of his life?

Chapter Eight
David: Beverly Hills Consigliore

In the spring of 2010, nearly one year after I left the boundaries of Taft's minimum-security prison camp, I appeared before California's Department of Real Estate. After a disgraceful departure from my career as a stockbroker at UBS, and before I reported to serve my sentence, I supported myself by selling real estate for the Calabasas office of Sotheby's. Upon my criminal conviction for securities fraud, the Department of Real Estate initiated action against my license to work as a real estate agent. My 2010 hearing represented an effort to persuade the Department of Real Estate that despite the bad decisions I had made as a stockbroker, I should not be precluded from the privilege of earning a living by selling real estate.

To testify on my behalf as character witnesses, I brought a team of three professionals. The team included Roger Ewing and Ernie Wish, who were partners in the Sotheby's office, and Sam Pompeo, one of the office's most respected agents. The team lauded efforts I had made to redeem the bad decisions that led to my troubles with the criminal justice system and they moved me to tears with their willingness to vouch for my good character.

The lawyer who represented the Department of Real Estate, on the other hand, was less impressed. "I have no doubt that Mr. Paperny can earn a livable wage in many careers," the lawyer said, "but selling real estate should not be one of those choices." I didn't go in to the meeting with high expectations of having my license to sell real estate reinstated, but the hearing gave me another wake up call to the lasting consequences that plagued those who violated the codes of ethics and professional conduct.

In failing to make honesty, prudence, and the other virtues that constituted good character a part of my every decision, I invited lifelong consequences. Regardless of how many good deeds I tried to sow in society, daily reminders would keep my criminal conviction as an indelible blemish on my life. I was living with that reality despite my having been released from prison for longer than a full year, and I expected to live with it forever.

When I engaged in deceptions as a stockbroker, I did not anticipate all the lingering influences of my shortsightedness. I did not consider how it would victimize others. I did not consider how it would wipe out every penny I had ever made, both legally and illegally. I did not consider how those who loved me would suffer. And I certainly did not consider the fatal blow the deception would bring to the professional career I had worked so hard to build.

Professor Bob Scharlach, a professor of tax accounting at USC, was one of my mentors and baseball coaches when I was a university student. After my release from prison, Professor Scharlach extended the privilege of allowing me to share my story with his students. As I had once done, they were diligently preparing for professional careers. While standing in ignominy before those students with so much promise, I expressed my admiration, telling them that I wished for a do-over so I could join them. But life did not offer do-overs. Once we crossed ethical lines we had to live with the consequences. To emphasize my point, I shared my own story, and I also told them about David, a client I was working with who was about to begin serving a five-year term in federal prison.

Like the students in Professor Scharlach's class were working toward, David had earned his undergraduate degree in accounting. He graduated from UC Berkley in the early 1980's, then continued his education at the University of San Francisco, where he earned an MBA with a specialty in tax. From USF David enrolled in the law school at Stanford, concluding his formal education with a JD in 1987.

Armed with such stellar academic credentials and promise, the recruiters at what was then one of the big-eight accounting firms were eager to bring David on board. He sharpened his skills by working 100-hour workweeks on audit teams for global corporations, but after seven years, David opted out to open a niche practice in Beverly Hills as a personal business manager for successful artists and executives in the entertainment industry.

Beginning his practice in 1994, David shifted his expertise from directly handling accounting, tax, or legal affairs to becoming more of a consigliore to his clients. He served as a personal counselor, overseeing all of his clients' financial and business decisions. By outsourcing their needs for professional services, David minimized his firm's staffing requirements. The accountants, lawyers, tax specialists, estate advisors, stockbrokers, real estate agents, and anyone else who provided professional services on behalf of David's clients reported directly to him. David's clients relied upon him to ensure all of their bills were paid and needs were met. They expected him to coordinate their purchases for automobiles, real estate, and in some cases, private jets. David took care of more modest requests as well, including reservations for dinners, hotels, or special events.

Chapter Eight

The stars that David represented earned substantial incomes. They did not want to be bothered with anything that was not directly related to their work or image, so they paid David well to oversee all business-related decisions, including their investments. David's problems with the law had their roots in one investment that he poured millions of his clients' dollars into.

David was in his mid 40's and for the time being he still lived in a magnificent Beverly Hills home with his wife, Laura. He was under pressure because part of his sanction required that he pay more than $18 million in restitution. While David reported to prison, Laura would bear the burden of selling the family home, settling a complicated bankruptcy, finding employment, and moving into affordable housing. David and I met at his house before the downsizing began, and I admired scores of gold-framed photographs that decorated the mahogany paneled walls of his home office. Those pictures were clearly taken in happier times, with David dressed in an elegant tuxedo, smiling with his arms embracing people whose faces would be recognized around the world.

"They were all like family to Laura and me," David said as I stood in front of the picture wall. "Now they wouldn't even take my calls."

"Tell me how it all fell apart. What was it that brought you down?"

"I selected investments for my clients," David said. "I considered them my responsibility, as my reputation was on the line. When one of the investments turned out to be an embarrassment, I stepped in, thinking I could salvage it. That decision only made matters worse. It's been a downward spiral ever since."

"What kind of investment was it?"

"Several years ago, in the late 1990s, I came across an investment opportunity through Tom, a colleague of mine." David leaned back in chair and took of his glasses as he told me the story. "The investment was in funding a factoring company. Internet and telephone companies were racking up tens of millions of dollars each month worth of credit card sales by selling sex. They operated adult-themed entertainment sites, 1-900 telephone numbers, that sort of thing. But once the bills came due, many of the customers tried to stop payment, stiffing the telephone and Internet companies that provided the service. Tom's factoring company offered a solution to the service providers. His company bought the receivables for pennies on the dollar, then went about collecting the funds."

"Okay, I understand."

"You say that as if I'm talking about a buck and half," David chuckled. "Tom was offering investors a fixed rate of return, a flat 15 percent, payable every month. I did the due diligence on behalf of my clients. The investment checked out. For 10 cents on the dollar the factoring company could purchase receivables in tranches of $10 million, $20 million, $50 million—whatever. Through my clients, I could provide the funds and bank on that steady fixed-income stream of 15 percent."

"Was Tom steady in disbursing the interest payments on the debt?"

"Like a Swiss clock," David said. "For years my clients could count on that attractive yield. But then Tom had a personal problem and I made the bad decision of stepping in to help."

"What was that?"

"Drugs. He got strung out. I don't know what kind of poison he was on...cocaine, meth, heroin, maybe all three. All I know was that he came to my office one day pleading for me to take over. Tom said his addictions were destroying his life and he was getting out, going on Safari, to Africa, India, Egypt, anywhere that he thought he could make a new start. Either I could take over the business or he was abandoning it."

David told me that he had acted rashly, foolishly. He had too much of his clients' money invested to let Tom simply abandon collections. Besides the millions of dollars on the line, David said his business was built on trust and discretion. His clients expected David to ensure their investments were sound and that their names were never tarnished by scandal. If word had gotten out that David had entrusted millions of dollars to a drug addict who presided over a business of questionable ethics, his reputation would have suffered, regardless of the yield the investment had been generating.

"I couldn't consider the failure option," David said. "I made a snap decision to take over."

"Did you confide in anyone?"

"I couldn't," David said. "There wasn't any time. I had to act. The only choice was either to take the reins completely or trust Tom to unravel the mess that I was suddenly and unexpectedly tangled up in. I drafted the necessary documents we both signed, I transferred accounts, and just like that," David snapped his fingers, "I was CEO of a factoring company. For the next few weeks I conducted an audit of the entire operation."

"So you took over ownership of the business without having to compensate Tom at all?"

"Tom took care of himself, and he did it through fraud. My audit revealed that he had absconded with $2 million dollars that I was suddenly on the hook to repay."

"What do you mean? Are you saying he simply took cash out?"

"The other way around," David said. "He never put the cash in, but he issued notes obligating the company to pay the fixed amount in interest every month."

"How? Who received the notes?"

"You see, I wasn't the only client who fed the factoring company with capital to invest. Tom had a network of professionals who either invested on behalf of their clients, as I did, or advised their clients of the returns and suggested they invest on their own. During the year prior to my taking control of the company, Tom accepted $2 million on behalf of the company and he issued notes to the investors. Those notes promised to pay a 15-percent annual interest rate. Supposedly," David went on to explain, "the company would use that $2 million to purchase a bundle of $20 million worth of receivables from a telephone company or Internet company. The factoring company's collection service would aggressively pursue settlements with customers, using the income from those settlements to pay the 15 percent yield and to bank a profit. But instead of using the $2 million to purchase the bundle of receivables, Tom instructed the investors to wire the funds to a separate offshore account that didn't have any ties to the factoring company. My audit revealed that the company I took responsibility for was obligated to pay the interest on the $2 million—and it carried the debt—but it didn't have the offsetting receivables."

When I asked how he responded to his discovery of the purloined funds, he told me that he transferred $2 million from his personal account to the factoring company. He purchased the receivables and allowed the factoring company to continue operations.

"I take it that you made a determination that the factoring company was a good investment," I said.

"It was a headache," David said, "a problem that I didn't need but one that I was trying to resolve, foolishly thinking I could unwind it quietly."

"So why did you put your own money into it?"

"I just wasn't thinking everything through." David sat shaking his head, combing fingers through thinning hair, defeated. "Clients relied on my discretion to protect them from scandal. The factoring venture had promise, but I wasn't set up to oversee its operations, not while simultaneously responding to clients with the personal attention they were entitled to receiving from me. I should have leveled with my clients from the outset, been honest about my being duped by Tom and worked to liquidate the factoring company. I lacked the courage, I guess, to own my mistake. Instead I kept it running, providing clients with monthly statements and interest payments that mischaracterized the company's balance sheet and financial health."

"If you were overseeing the financial affairs of your clients, and you were overseeing the affairs of the factoring company, how did your acts come to the attention of the authorities?"

"David scratched his scalp. I called the district attorney myself."

"What motivated you to make the call? Guilty conscience?"

"I suppose you're right," David said. "It was my guilty conscience. It began because I didn't feel right about my having transferred $2 million to shore up the factoring company without discussing the situation with Laura. We had been married for 12 years and what was mine was hers. If she had blown through $2 million without telling me about it I would have felt betrayed. I owed her the truth about the mess I'd created and what I had to done to solve it, so I told her."

"What was her response?"

"Laura wasn't upset about the money," David shrugged. "But when she asked whether I had done anything illegal, I had to tell her the truth. In altering financial records and covering up the ruse by creating inaccurate statements, my actions were fraudulent. Laura and I discussed it and agreed that I should contact authorities to come clean completely."

"And your clients," I asked, "What did you say to them?"

"I came clean with them also. The problems exploded, tearing my business apart in a matter of days. Clients hired new attorneys to represent them, and the prosecutors began their investigation. I cooperated completely, but the disruption froze the income stream from debt collections, causing the factoring company to fail. I've lost everything."

"So you pleaded guilty?"

David nodded. "I agreed to plead guilty to a single count of mail fraud. In exchange for my cooperation, the prosecutors agreed to a five-year sentence, but the judge also slammed me with an $18 million restitution order. We're in bankruptcy now, and the trustee is liquidating assets. My only hope is that once this ends, my cooperation in the investigation will help convince authorities to reinstate my licenses so I can work again."

David's guilty plea required him to declare in open court that he had committed the crime of mail fraud. He admitted to having used the mail "to send financial statements with the intent to convey false or misleading information." It was somewhat similar to the crime of securities fraud that I pleaded guilty to committing.

In working with David, my job was to help him prepare for the consequences that would follow his conviction. When David told me that he hoped his convictions for fraud would not preclude his ability to work as a lawyer or accountant again, it sounded as if he wanted a do-over. But as I told the students in Professor Scharlach's tax and accounting classes at USC, professionals who crossed ethical lines rarely received do-overs. I shared with David what I had learned through my preparations to persuade the California Department of Real Estate to reinstate my license.

Licensing agencies that governed such professions as real estate sales, securities, law, accounting, and so forth, considered an individual's character when determining whether the individual was fit to serve. A key question was whether the applicant for license had ever been convicted of a crime of "moral turpitude." Not being clear on what that term meant, I researched legal findings. The courts of California (as elsewhere), I was saddened to learn, held that any action taken with the intent to defraud involved moral turpitude.

I did not consider the consequences of those actions that led to my problems with the criminal justice system. But as I was trying to build an argument that might allow me to retain my license to sell real estate, I had to come to terms with what courts had ruled. I couldn't undo my past. The courts concluded that if an individual's conduct ever involved "deceit, graft, trickery, or dishonest means," it involved moral turpitude and thus rendered a person unfit to hold a professional license.

"But you still put yourself through the trouble and expense of making a case before the Department of Real Estate," David was clinging to hope. "You must have thought that there was something you could do to get your license back."

"I went through the motions," I agreed. "Yet I knew what I was up against. I had committed a crime as a stockbroker, not a real estate agent. And I've worked hard to redeem myself through honesty, transparency, and community service as many character witnesses testified. Despite the good deeds I tried to contribute, I understood that the Department of Real Estate would be unlikely to ignore the character blemishes that led to my troubles with the law. I had hopes, but I went into my hearing with the understanding that my criminal conviction was going to present a hurdle that might prove insurmountable."

David continued making arguments suggesting that he wasn't yet willing to accept the lifelong consequences that accompanied convictions for any kind of fraud. My role was to remove the ostrich-like delusions, to prepare him in the best way I could for the challenges ahead. But part of my ongoing redemption was to share experiences like those of David's and mine with students and professionals who kept their licenses in good standing. Such experiences, I was convinced, would provide solid reasons to confront all dilemmas with courage and to respect the value of an honest reputation.

Chapter Eight Questions

1. What can a person convicted of a white-collar crime do to restore good character?

2. In what ways does serving a prison term equate with justice?

3. How should society respond to white-collar offenders who satisfied the justice system?

Chapter Nine
Derick's Bribery Charge

Professor Bruce Zucker invited me to speak to his business law classes at California State University in Northridge. My memories of studying business law were that the course introduced us to such concepts as the necessary elements of a contract, corporate structures, laws governing employment, and so forth. I intended to enlighten the Cal-State Northridge students on more practical dilemmas they may face once they entered the workforce. My presentation would focus on consequences that could follow personal failure.

The type of failure I wanted to describe wasn't the type they were used to hearing about. Rather than discussing poor job performance or professional errors, I wanted to speak openly about how people who considered themselves good citizens were seduced by abandoning ethical principles. I understood that Professor Zucker's students worked hard to earn credentials that would lead to fulfilling careers and that they looked forward to joining the workforce as promising professionals. They couldn't contemplate themselves engaging in theft or participating in the types of "street crime" that led local news broadcasts every day. *But what about more esoteric crimes?* I stood before them to talk about the pressures and the rationalizations that would come to them, as their professional responsibilities—or capacities—increased.

I've heard some people define an individual's ethics by the way a person acted when others weren't watching. Many professionals worked with levels of discretion that kept their decisions and the reasons for making their decisions private. When I was a stockbroker, for example, overseeing hundreds of millions of dollars in client assets at UBS, no one would question how I executed trades. I didn't always act transparently, especially when opportunities opened that would line my pockets with extra income. Since no one would know other than the individual who made the underhanded payment to me, I didn't consider the payment anyone else's business. In reality, my actions in accepting the "kickback" violated ethical codes, and quite frankly, accepting kickbacks may have violated some laws as well. I shrugged off such concerns, ignoring inherent conflicts that were at the root of my decisions with rationalizations that I was doing my job and that no one was being hurt.

With a barrage of news reports describing the paucity of ethics within the culture of Wall Street, my admission of accepting kickbacks didn't surprise any of the bright students in Professor Zucker's class. I stood ready and willing to respond to their questions about my motivations, but the real teachable moment didn't come from my experiences. Instead, I got the students to listen when I told them about my conversations with Derick. Whereas graft within the stockbroker community wasn't so shocking, Derick's background of service to our country suggested that he would have honed a more reliable moral compass. In sharing what I learned from Derick, I shared how anyone who disregarded the importance of making values-based decisions could become susceptible to temptations that could destroy a lifelong pursuit of honor, integrity, and reputation.

Derick grew up in Nevada with aspirations of becoming a soldier. His cousin served in the Air Force and regaled him with exciting stories about traveling the world, about training experiences, about the camaraderie. After graduating high school, Derick enlisted with hopes of maturing and preparing himself for life's challenges.

He completed boot camp in Kelly Air Force Base, Texas, then continued training to become a supply and services specialist. Derick's hard work and grasp of logistics led to his assignment in a squadron at Travis Air Force Base, in Northern California. Later, Derick transferred to a coveted spot at the base in Aviano, Italy. Through hard work, discipline, and study, he rapidly advanced his rank from airman to sergeant.

Derick's tour of Italy concluded about the same time as his initial three-year commitment to the Air Force, but Derick said that he found personal value in all that the military stood for so he reenlisted for another six years. The reenlistment brought him to Charleston Air Force Base in South Carolina, where he became a part of the supply and services squadron. Wanting to advance further with the military, Derick completed his college degree and received training in logistics while on a one-year tour in Korea. He then returned to Aviano where leadership training and discipline led to his further advancement in rank to staff sergeant and eventually to Master Chief.

As a logistician, Derick's responsibilities required him to coordinate supply lines for troops in various parts of the world. Thousands of soldiers depended upon his judgment and his ability to anticipate the unexpected. In addition to becoming fluent with various computer application systems, Derick understood that his primary asset was his network of contacts. The job required him to build trust in relationships, as through trust he could expand both his sphere of influence as well as perform his duties with more efficiency.

Derick's identity became wrapped up with his need to build a reputation as a man who served his country with honor. To that end, when his second enlistment expired, Derick applied to officer training school and he was accepted. He agreed to continue his career with the Air Force for another 10 years, and graduated with the rank of second lieutenant. After a few years, Derick's responsibilities increased to the point where he was promoted to Major where he oversaw supply lines to American military troops throughout the entire Middle East.

Derick's duty of ensuring that supplies and munitions flowed despite continuous threat of attack by enemy forces required him to employ creativity and ingenuity on a grand scale. Despite an abundance of classroom and theoretical training, Derick worked in a war zone. His superior expected him to use discretion, to cultivate contacts, to find ways to complete his job by whatever means were necessary. As an officer, Derick was a professional with influence over billions of dollars worth of supplies every month. I met Derick just after he pleaded guilty to bribery charges that resulted in an 18-month sentence. He was about to self-surrender to federal prison.

"So how long in total did you serve in the Air Force," I asked.

"I completed 25 years but I was expecting to serve another 10 years. The military was my life."

"Can you tell me about the pressures that led to your crime?"

Since Derick had pleaded guilty, I suggested that he might derive some therapeutic value in talking about his decisions. We spoke at a Starbucks in Los Angeles. While sipping coffee, Derick looked down at the table, his buzz cut as precise as his military bearing. "I hope you don't feel ashamed," I ventured. "We're all human beings and we all have made decisions that we wish we could take back. I certainly have. The answer—for me at least—has been acknowledging my weaknesses and committing myself to do better."

"A war zone is a crazy place." Derick began. "But that's not a valid excuse for the decisions I made. I'm not some gullible kid, green to the ways of the world. I just got sucked in," he shook his head slowly, then took a sip from his mug, "doing things I knew that I shouldn't be doing."

"You said that you pleaded guilty to bribery. How did it start?"

"It started with curiosity," Derick said. "Wasn't it curiosity that killed the cat? The curiosity led to temptations. Just a gradual slide. Then I was in, caught in the trap of corruption that I had trained all my life to avoid. I just lost my way."

"How? What started it?"

"My job was to ensure that troops received the supplies they needed. Without supplies they couldn't accomplish their mission. But in the theatre of war, getting supplies to remote locations wasn't as easy as driving to the local Wal-Mart. We had to navigate around land mines, sniper fire, suicide bombers, and unexpected disasters. Improvised explosive devices could strike at any given moment, but none of that would interfere with the continuous need for supplies. My job was to fulfill the mission regardless of the threats, and as an officer that responsibility required me to understand both the terrain and the locals who had influence over the terrain."

Derick explained to me how his position as an officer with responsibilities across the entire theatre of operations brought him to the attention of enterprising businessmen who controlled companies selling billions of dollars worth of goods and services to the Air Force.

"It all began subtly," he said, "with an invitation to dinner. I knew that I was being courted but I'm a poker player. I was curious to see how the hand would play out and I accepted."

"Were you invited by an American or someone from the Middle East?"

"My initial contact was with a Saudi who was part of the royal family. His company distributed cleaning supplies and other products across the region. We met for dinner the first time in a palatial home he kept in Iraq. I felt totally out of place."

"Why? Was it a large gathering?"

"Not large. Just him, five exquisitely beautiful young women, and me. The setting was ostentatious, with butlers and servants. I was a meat and potatoes guy who didn't fit in with the perfumed atmosphere, the formality. But the host was gracious, a real charmer and I was intrigued, like a kid flipping through the pages of his first Playboy.

"Did he make you an offer of some kind?"

"Oh, no," Derick chuckled. "These were high stakes and my host wasn't new to the game. He was a roller, a player. All he was doing was laying it all out for me to see, showing the perks that could come with his friendship. The man showed real interest in my background. When I told him that I had grown up in Nevada, he told me about a house he owned in Lake Tahoe and promised an invitation the next time he was in the U.S.

"Did you discuss any business at all?"

"Not that first night. We just enjoyed dinner, got to know one another a little bit."

"Then there wasn't any violation of law, right?"

Derick explained to me the intricacies of law. He was an officer in the United States Air Force. Under Title 18 of the U.S. Criminal Code, Section 302, that title distinguished him as a public official. Accordingly, special laws (having to do with Chapter 11 of the Title 18 criminal code) applied to Derick, especially those concerning bribery, graft, and conflicts of interest.

"I wouldn't say that there wasn't *any* violation. I mean, I understood that as an officer I had discretion and influence over billions of dollars in goods and services. My mind was supposed to focus exclusively on the needs of our troops. Those of us who had such positions were required to abide by strict rules that would put a cap on the value of services or goods or gifts we received. My meeting with the prince may have begun with a dinner at his home, but I shouldn't have been there. I regret that I didn't follow military protocol and refrain from socializing with someone who wanted to curry favor with me. The rules governing conflicts of interest existed for a reason. I knew what I was getting into—I'm not stupid—and the dinner made me want to walk a little closer to the fire, to see how he would court me."

"Okay. So you left the dinner without discussing any business. What happened next?"

"I left the dinner with an invitation to another event and of course my curiosity compelled me to accept."

"Did he invite you back to his house?"

"Not the second time," Derick said. "He invited me to a gathering that he hosted in a luxury hotel. When I walked in I met seven or eight other Middle Eastern businessmen, all sheiks or members of the royal family who owned businesses that supplied the military. Some wore the flashy robes with headwear, others were in tailored suits. The ratio of striking young women to men must have been three to one. The women may have

111

mingled with grace and elegance but my host assured me that they were there to please me. He said that the adjoining suite belonged to me for the weekend and that I should enjoy it."

"Any business discussed," I asked.

"Nope. Purely social. Again, he was laying out the spread, showing the vastness and influence of his wealth. Before he introduced me to the other businessmen at the gathering, he extolled their importance, telling me how much they controlled and how each of them was enthusiastic about meeting an American officer. I could see what was going on, and that meeting clearly crossed lines. I wasn't having dinner with a 'friend' in his home. I was in a hotel, allowing foreigners to wine and dine me despite my duty of overseeing contractual performance of their businesses with the United States. I didn't have an excuse. I knew that I was crossing a line but I was intrigued with the illusion of power."

"Besides that," I pointed out, "you probably weren't so eager to turn down the offer of a prepaid hotel suite that you could share with an attractive young woman."

"Humph," Derick snorted. "Or three young women! But the truth was that I shouldn't have gone to that party in the first place. I knew better. I could lie to myself all day that I wasn't doing anything wrong. In fact, I tried to justify my acceptance of the invitation in my mind with my responsibilities of nurturing local contracts which would help me keep supply lines open. As I look back now, I know those were only excuses."

"What about the rules of that country," I asked. "I mean, you were in Iraq, not the United States. Were there any laws in those countries about the exchange of gifts in the course of government business?"

"I wasn't only in Iraq," Derick pointed out. "Like I said, my responsibilities covered the entire theatre of operations—wherever we had military personnel in the region. I was in Iraq, Afghanistan, Kuwait, all the way to the horn of Africa. The laws of those countries weren't supposed to govern my conduct. I was an officer in the United States Air Force. My allegiance was to the U.S. and I was supposed to act honorably. I knew that. Like I said, the power just sucked me in."

"Well, did the prince expect you to reciprocate for all the attention he was lavishing on you? Did there come a time when he made an actual bribe?"

"Every week he invited me to one event or another, always peppering the event with seductive women. If we didn't get together he would arrange something else, like a hotel suite for me to use. Two or three months of this dance continued before he asked me to reciprocate. By the time he did, I was thoroughly corrupted and ready to comply."

"What happened?"

"I was in Kuwait when he invited me to a meeting in an office he kept there. After some smooth praise about how my reputation for honesty and character was well known throughout the region, and how he would not consider offending me, he handed me a stack of ten requests for proposals. 'Would you do me a favor of looking through there, he asked? I'd like your opinion.' That was the moment of truth."

"Why? What was so different?"

"Well, he wasn't simply entertaining me with women and wine. I looked through a few of the documents and I knew exactly what he was asking. Those RFPs represented contracts that, as an officer, I would oversee. For me to discuss any aspect of them with a potential bidder was tantamount to official corruption, and I knew it."

"So what did you say?"

"I just flipped through a few of the pages, then set them back down on the table. I told him I would have to think about it, that I couldn't make a decision right then. We both understood the gravity of what he was asking me to do. He was very calm, told me of course he understood that I was a man of decency and that he respected me, that I should take time to think. I also emphasized that my position didn't authorize me to decide who would receive the contract. My job, I explained, was to ensure the supplies arrived to the troops on time. He knew all of that. He made clear that he knew the protocol. He named my superiors, the officers who would issue the contract. All he hoped that I could provide, however, was a recommendation to assure anyone who might ask that his company provided excellent service."

"What was the value of the contracts that he was after," I asked.

"There were 10 RFPs," Derick said. The smallest was in the $50 million range; the largest was more than $500 million. He handed me a steel attaché case before I left his office, telling me it was a small token of gratitude to show his appreciation. I shouldn't have considered it. But I paused, looked at it. He watched me. I opened the case. There were ten stacks, all hundreds, new crisp bills. The paper bands holding the stacks together indicated each was worth $10,000. I think they must have been perfumed because they sure smelled sweet," Derick laughed. "I should have pushed the case away. Instead, I walked out from that office on shaky legs, but with the briefcase firmly in my grip."

Derick sat across from me describing the disgust he felt with himself for having accepted the funds. Although he lacked the power to decide who would receive contracts, when his host named all of Derick's superiors, the chain of command, and the complete internal procedures, it was clear that groundwork was being laid. The contractors shouldn't have even had access to the RFPs. Others were involved with this methodical plan of corruption, and Derick was being paid to provide cover. With billions of dollars funding the war, Derick said he had reason to believe the corruption originated at the highest levels of our government. Still, he expressed shame for having sold the honor and reputation he had devoted a lifetime to building.

In the end, the decisions Derick made would affect more than his conscience. His tour of duty in the Middle East concluded with his reassignment to the United States. Despite being stationed outside the theatre of war, considerations from the government contractors continued to flow his way.

Derick was returning home from an all-expense paid ski trip in the Rockies. He and his three guests had enjoyed the trip. But the good times cooled when Derick fielded a phone call from an officer with the military's criminal investigation division. Officials in Iraq had intercepted a suitcase filled with currency that another officer was sending home. When officials interrogated that officer, he confessed to his participation in contract manipulations. The admission gave the criminal investigators a new thread to follow, and the thread led to Derick. He pleaded guilty to bribery charges.

"Listen Justin," Derick told me, "I didn't contact you because I needed help in preparing for 18 months of imprisonment. I've been in combat, driven through roads littered with land mines. Prison doesn't mean anything to me, whether I'm locked alone in a concrete bunker or sent to one of those white-collar camps. I called to talk with you about the real punishment, and that's the continuous assault on my conscience. I don't know how to put this episode behind me. I don't have a wife or children. Reputation was what I lived for, and that's gone—dishonored. How's a guy supposed to cope with that?"

Derick lived for honor and reputation—devoted his life to such virtues—yet even he succumbed to the same type of temptations that brought down so many people who never expected such falls. I may not have had a military career, but I could identify with the self-loathing that followed the realization and acceptance of my wrongdoing. What Derick didn't understand was the acceptance and a desire to do better was the essential beginning of the healing process. In response to Derick's question I described the daily exercises and commitments I made to live an ethical life.

"But is that going to be enough?" he asked. "Do you think that I'll ever put this behind me?"

"The truth is," I told Derick, "I work at it every day. I write about my crime; I speak about my crime; I talk about my crime. All of those activities represent a part of my continuing journey to become a better man. I don't know whether we ever put our bad decisions behind us, but I know that by considering them, owning them, and learning from them, we can work toward redeeming ourselves, toward finding peace."

When I met with Derick I had been home from prison for a year. Despite the efforts to reconcile with society and with my conscience, I struggled for a time coping with some of the realties that come with having a felony conviction. Whenever I would meet new people on social occasions (especially women), I felt awkward divulging that I had been in prison. That changed after I met the basketball legend, Kareem Abdul Jabbar. Kareem was a friend of my father, Bernie. The three of us had dinner one night together and I told my story. Kareem listened. Then he told me about a lesson he had learned from Coach John Wooden when he was playing at UCLA.

"Any man can make a bad decision," Kareem said, "regardless of his status in life, but what makes a man great is when he recognized his wrongs, then worked to become better."

Kareem looked at me directly and nodded. Then he reached his hand across the table to shake mine. With a firm grip, he said, "welcome home. You have made your father very proud by the way you've accepted responsibility and by working to become better, and I want you to know that I respect you." My father had tears in his eyes, and at that moment, seeing that I had made my father proud, I found new strength. It was a special moment for me, a turning point, the type that I assured Derick he would experience by working to become better every day.

Chapter Nine Questions

1. How does an individual's response to temptation change with an increase in authority or discretion?

2. What should guide an individual's decisions when laws and customs from one country where one does business differ from those of the U.S.?

3. What exercises can organizations offer to encourage individuals to work toward becoming better every day?

Chapter Ten
Jeff's Cash Structuring

Through an invitation from James Sysco, professor of law and ethics at King's College, I had the privilege of speaking to students, faculty, and the academic community of Wilkes-Barre, Pennsylvania. Many of those in my audience, I understood, taught business courses, studied toward business careers, or led Pennsylvania businesses. They would expect my presentation to describe what I learned as a consequence of my travails with the criminal justice system.

What kind of pressures, influences, or motivations dragged people from their positions of honor to the depths of infamy, despite all they had invested into their educations, their careers, and their communities? The community leaders and future community leaders in the audience, I expected, would rightfully consider themselves good citizens and the thought of their ever becoming tangled into problems with the criminal justice system would seem surreal, like something out of a Salvador Dali painting, or like growing a third arm. As far as they were concerned, such possibilities simply didn't apply to them, and I understood.

Similarly, I once mistook my educational credentials and career as validation that I was a member of society in perpetual good standing. What I didn't appreciate then was how the daily decisions I made would continue to determine who I was as an individual. Through my experiences I came to accept that we never truly "arrived." Instead, we were more like works in progress that were continuously tested and susceptible to decisions that could bring dramatic change in a hurry. For example, one year I was a UBS stockbroker on the rise, a big brother who mentored at-risk youths, a good son and citizen. The next year I was a convicted felon, a federal prisoner, a disgrace to my community. The journey through life, I learned, was like crossing a high wire. Bad decisions could drop us from zenith to nadir in an instant, as so many citizens discovered. Continuously working to strengthen our ethical cores—experience convinced me—was the surest way to keep balance. Without that balance our lives could fall apart.

Those in my audience at King's College, I understood, may or may not have identified with my descriptions of the toxic triangle that led so many, myself included, into fraudulent behavior. Pressure, capacity, and rationalization influenced the gradual ethical slide that led to my conviction for securities fraud, but the professors, students, and business leaders who listened attentively to descriptions of my downfall could not envision themselves becoming involved in a deception that rose to the level of criminal misconduct. That was why I wanted to tell them about what I learned from Jeff. His was a story that illustrated more clearly the importance of practicing honesty in every decision, every day.

Jeff and I were sitting at a booth in the comfortable clubhouse after a round of 18 holes as he told me his story. He was tall, African-American, in remarkably good physical condition for a man in his mid-50s. Jeff served as the chief executive officer of a publicly traded manufacturing company. Among his numerous responsibilities (to shareholders, his board of directors, his employees, his clients, and his community) as the CEO of a publicly traded company, Jeff had obligations to the federal government. As part of legislation known as Sarbanes-Oxley, in 2002 the US Congress added sections 1348, 1349, and 1350 to Title 18 of the US criminal code. Those laws provided stiff penalties of up to 25 years imprisonment for crimes related to securities fraud, including "failure of corporate officers to certify financial reports."

"I had served as CFO of my company for seven years before our board offered me the CEO position," Jeff told me, "so I was intimately familiar with all of our accounting procedures. I didn't have any reservations about certifying the financial reports we filed with the SEC. I knew we kept pristine records—conservative—because I had put the systems and procedures in place myself, and I worked closely with my handed-picked CFO."

"Then why didn't you want to cooperate with the FBI?" I asked.

"I did," Jeff said, "but they didn't like what I had to say. The FBI wasn't investigating my company. It was after our auditors. The agents wanted me to provide some type of damaging evidence they could use against our accounting firm. But whatever the accounting firm may have done with other clients didn't concern me; I didn't know anything. The accountants audited our records, and I was confident they were clean, that we didn't have anything to hide. The agents didn't want to hear that."

"And so what happened?"

"Harassment. That's what happened. The agents pestered me beyond my ability to tolerate. I just didn't have time—didn't want to take the time to play with them. They were insinuating that they would find something if they kept looking—antitrust violations, employment issues—any threat that would pressure me to provide dirt on our accountants. I lawyered up to minimize the seemingly continuous interruptions. The FBI didn't like that, but I wasn't going to continue ignoring the threats. As far as I was concerned, the accountants had done a thorough job. I didn't do anything wrong, so I instructed our law firm to keep the agents off my back."

Jeff expressed absolute confidence that he had presided over all professional responsibilities honestly and ethically. He knew his company operated within the law, and because of his leadership he didn't think the agents could bully him. As CEO, Jeff said that he was an open book, completely transparent, accountable to his board and the company's shareholders without anything to hide. His personal life, on the other hand, wasn't quite so flawless. He had been married for 18 years, but when his wife discovered that Jeff was carrying on an adulterous affair, she initiated contentious divorce proceedings. A battle over financial issues was escalating.

"Obviously," Jeff said in describing how he became the target of a criminal investigation, "I had interests outside of my company. Over the years my wife and I had acquired substantial investments in real estate, equities, and bonds. Those assets were easy to value, not a problem as far as the divorce proceedings were concerned. But I had also made some investments in start-up companies, a few of which were doing quite well. It was an agreement I had with one of those companies that tripped me up, got me into trouble that I didn't even know existed."

"What was that?"

"Cash structuring," Jeff said.

"What's that," I asked, "something to do with taxes?"

Jeff shook his head. "Not at all. I paid my taxes, all of them. Cash structuring was an entirely different animal, but one that bit. Because of it I'm going to prison for 15 months."

Jeff was clearly troubled that indiscretions in his personal life had abruptly ended his professional career and sullied his reputation as an honest man, a man of high integrity. The reality that his actions had risen to the level of criminal behavior stunned him, and he couldn't believe that he would soon self-surrender to a federal prison.

"I was involved with a young woman" Jeff spoke quietly, his elbow on the varnished wood table, three fingers supporting his head. "I'm not proud of having deceived my wife, but those things could happen when a man fell off track. It wasn't unusual, not the first or last time a man would feel invigorated by the attention of a beautiful woman. She brought out a second life in me, and I succumbed to the temptation."

Jeff explained how he supplemented his mistress's income for the two years of their relationship. One of the start-up companies he had funded provided Jeff with $9,500 a month in compensation. Although a considerable sum, at that stage in Jeff's career the amount wasn't significant and he relied upon it to fund his illicit affair. Rather than depositing the $9,500 check he received each month from the start-up company into the personal account he kept jointly with his wife, Jeff endorsed each check and instructed his bank to hand him cash instead. He referred to it as "play money," and said he provided it to his mistress as she saw fit.

Pursuant to Title 31 of the U.S. code section 5313 (a), financial institutions must report all currency transactions that involved more than $10,000.

"I didn't want to trouble with the currency transaction reports," Jeff said. "Truthfully, I wasn't so keen on leaving a string of records that my wife could later tie into a noose and hang around my neck. That was why I had the company cut checks that were less than $10,000. My banker told me that as long as the checks didn't exceed $10,000, the law didn't require me to file the CTR."

"Regardless of the CTR, wasn't the $9,500 taxable income?" I asked.

"Of course it was taxable, and I reported. I wasn't keeping secrets from the IRS. But when considering salary and investments, the $9,500 represented less than 10 percent of my total income. That wasn't going to stand out on the comprehensive tax filings my wife and I filed every year. She signed those forms without concern. If I would have deposited the $9,500 checks into the bank accounts I jointly held with my wife, on the other hand, I would have exposed myself to questions from her that I wouldn't have wanted to answer. By simply cashing the checks, I thought I was protecting myself—but from my wife, not the IRS."

"So what happened? Did your wife's divorce lawyers catch you cashing the checks?"

"Nope. It was the FBI."

"If you were reporting the money as taxable income, why would the FBI be concerned with what you were doing with your money?"

"It was the same agents who were pressuring me to feed them information that might incriminate our auditors. I didn't have anything to say. First I brushed them off, then my lawyers took more aggressive actions to keep the agents from interfering with my time. The FBI doesn't like being stonewalled. When they couldn't get to me at the office, they started looking into my personal life."

Inquiries into Jeff's personal life led them to Facebook, the popular social networking Web site. They found the page his mistress kept, and since it featured pictures of Jeff, the agents decided to question her. They knocked on her front door and flashed their badges. Their presence alone intimidated her. When the agents asked the woman how she could afford such a lavish residence and expensive car when she wasn't working, she told them that Jeff provided it. They pressed with the questions and learned that Jeff gave her cash to pay her bills every month.

"It wasn't that she was saying anything to try and hurt me," Jeff said. "She was just responding to their questions truthfully. When the agents asked whether she declared the money I gave her as taxable income, she said yes."

"So what was the problem?"

"The agents dug further once they heard about my giving her $9,500 in cash every month. Wanting to know where I was getting the cash, the agents flashed their badges at my bank. That's where they learned about my cashing the $9,500 check every month."

"But I don't understand the problem," I shrugged. From what Jeff was describing I hadn't heard anything that I thought could be construed as a crime. The money belonged to him and he paid taxes on all of his earnings. It seemed as if he should have been able to use his money as he saw fit.

"I didn't know I had a problem either," Jeff said. "Then my lawyer called me. He told me that I was going to prison. It turns out that there was a law against my cashing checks without filing a cash transaction report."

Title 31 of the US code, section 5324, prohibits "structuring [cash] transactions to evade [the] reporting requirement." That statute provides for a penalty of up to five years imprisonment for those who "structure" transactions, as Jeff did, by cashing checks that were just under the $10,000 reporting requirement.

"Wait a minute," I was still confused. "I thought you said that the banker specifically told you that as long as the checks were for less than $10,000, the law didn't require you to file the cash transaction report."

"That's exactly what I told my lawyer. But the lawyer said that since bank employees weren't official representatives of the government, the banker's assurances were not going to provide a valid defense."

"What if you had been cashing checks for $5,000? Would that have been a crime?" I was shaking my head, wondering how many citizens were oblivious to the many types of behaviors that could lead to trouble with the criminal justice system.

"My lawyer wasn't misleading me," Jeff said. "He showed me the federal statutes. Then he showed me cases that illustrated how courts have interpreted the law if anyone attempted to structure cash transactions with the intention of avoiding the bank's filing of a currency transaction report, that person was committing a crime. Since the government had copies of all the checks I cashed, and since the pattern clearly showed my intention of avoiding the CTR, I was guilty."

Upon advice of counsel, Jeff agreed to plead guilty to the felony charge of cash structuring in exchange for leniency at sentencing. His judge imposed a 15-month sentence, and I spoke with Jeff about what he could expect from his prison experience. One drawback from his felony conviction, among many, was that it ended his career as a chief executive officer of a publicly traded corporation.

The magnitude of Jeff's loss was obvious. As I relayed his story to the leaders and future leaders at King's College in Pennsylvania, I emphasized the ancillary consequences that accompanied a felony conviction. Although those in my audience may not have felt susceptible to the fraud triangle of pressure, capacity, and rationalization (and thus vulnerable to making the kinds of bad decisions that led to my imprisonment), by sharing Jeff's chilling story I could provide practical reasons to live honestly at all times.

Jeff had earned his accounting degree and his MBA from Pennsylvania's prestigious Wharton school. He understood corporate codes well, and he also understood the personal investment necessary to rise through various career challenges that would deliver the coveted position of chief executive officer. As the leader of his company, Jeff oversaw a professional workforce of more than 1,500 people and revenues that exceeded $5 billion. He felt so confident that his business stewardship complied with the highest ethical standards that FBI agents couldn't shake him. When they came inquiring with what he perceived as subtle pressures, he responded from a position of strength rather than weakness.

Jeff's weakness, it turned out, came from flaws in his personal life rather than his professional life. Yet they were weaknesses just the same. He would suffer consequences, I knew, that would extend far beyond the length of his confinement. Although he couldn't comprehend how spending his own lawfully earned income could lead to imprisonment, as we sat in that clubhouse talking about the challenges to come, he understood how dishonesty at any time could derail a lifetime of good works.

In today's evolving society, I reminded my audience at King's college, the viral spreading of information through social networking sites like Facebook and Twitter and LinkedIn provided tangible new reasons to appreciate the importance of leading honest and transparent lives. Jeff cashed checks as part of a strategy to betray his wife's trust—not to break the law. Nevertheless, he doubted whether the FBI would have discovered the crime of his "cash structuring" had it not been for Facebook postings by his mistress. Although Jeff was of an older generation that wasn't in synch with technology, law enforcement relied upon it to bring his actions to the justice of 15 months imprisonment.

Technology would only continue to advance. Law enforcement was continuously relying upon it to develop their crime-detecting capabilities. Search techniques could provide resources to recognize faces or cull incriminating data from digital files. Advanced cell phones, blogs, and other technology made every citizen an investigative reporter whether that person knew it or not. Individuals may have the abilities to control their actions, but with digital recordings memorializing them all, people had an entirely new set of practical reasons to behave in ways that comported with the highest standards of ethics. Jeff's was a message of timely importance, and I hoped my audience at Kings' College grasped all of its implications.

Chapter Ten Questions

1. How do ethics in professional life relate to personal life?

2. In what ways does technology expose all that we think, say, and do?

3. Why would a commitment to complete honesty and integrity have made Jeff's ignorance of esoteric cash-structuring laws irrelevant?

Chapter Eleven
Susan's Efforts to Help a Client

Despite the completion of my sentence in August of 2009, the sanctions my judge imposed upon me included a three-year term of supervised release. While under supervised release, a United States Probation Officer would monitor my activities. In order to travel outside the Los Angeles area, I would need his permission. The probation officer would keep tabs on where I lived, with whom I associated, how I earned a living, and monitor compliance with my financial obligation to pay a $234,418 settlement the judge imposed as part of my criminal sanction. Those restrictions and interferences didn't trouble me because of my commitment to lead a transparent life.

This commitment to truth and correctness was not a part of my past. As I've written before, I used to be a liar. My willingness to lie was a necessary component of white-collar crime. The irony was that while living as the embodiment of deceit, I didn't consider my actions as being wrong or inconsistent with self-perceptions of my essential goodness as a human being. Readings in Machiavelli suggested that while living in a corrupt world, success required a person to master the art of deception. I was deluded into believing that by lying I could get ahead, and getting ahead was what I was all about.

With his theory of consequentialism, the ethicist John Stuart Mill wrote about the ends justifying the means. I once misinterpreted that theory. If earning more money was my end goal, then I didn't consider what I would have to do to reach that goal, including selling my morals. As long as the price made the decisions worthwhile, selling my morals wasn't such a stretch. Rather than living righteously, the question became how much would it take for me to abandon key concepts such as honesty and integrity.

Before I surrendered to prison, an awkward conversation clarified what honesty meant. I spoke with Neil Weinberg, a senior editor and journalist at *Forbes* who wrote extensively about white-collar crime. When Neil asked why I lied and cheated, I told him that what happened to me could happen to anyone. He rightfully took umbrage at my response. "It could never happen to me," Neil asserted. "I would never lie or cheat to get ahead, regardless of the payoff, regardless of whether I thought I could get away with it."

Neil's comment stayed with me, and I credit him as being one of the role models who inspired me to change. I admired his self-assurance, his certainty that he would always make decisions that were consistent with his strong sense of ethics. Whereas I was weakened and abashed by my conviction of lying and cheating, Neil's code of ethics endowed him with transparency. I admired the virtue, and in the spring of 2010, I got a sense of how empowering it was.

In early 2010 my accountant brought welcome news. As a consequence of the 2009 economic stimulus legislation, I was entitled to a five-figure refund of taxes that I had previously paid. The refund would bring a financial windfall, as I hadn't been expecting it. What's more, I wouldn't have to do anything other than sign a form to receive the check. And since it was a tax refund rather than new taxable income, my understanding was the conditions of my release wouldn't obligate me to disclose the refund to my probation officer. My previous mindset would have driven a decision to cash the check and use the funds as I saw fit. The commitment to transparency that role models like Neil Weinberg inspired, however, compelled me to reveal the refund to my probation officer. My forthrightness took him by surprise, I sensed, and in that moment I felt the strength of character that came with being an honest man.

What did it take for someone to sell his or her morals? Since my transformation I committed to living as an honest man, determined to prove myself worthy of the trust that societal leaders like Neil Weinberg, Walt Pavlo, Jr., and Mark Whitacre placed in me. But there was a time when an envelope stuffed with a crisp, bonded stack of $10,000 could cause me to ignore some irregular trading patterns in an account I managed; a monthly commission check of $50,000 could induce me to ignore outright fraud.

How about others? Some people with whom I spoke in my consulting practice shared the pressure points that led to their demise. For most it was money, the lure and temptation to rake it in easily. For Susan, a CPA, the slide began with a simple aversion to saying no to her clients.

"I was never a people pleaser," Susan told me. We met in her West LA office. She sat across from me in a high-backed leather chair, meticulously dressed, but lines in her face revealed the stress she was enduring. "I began my career at Arthur Andersen, and it didn't take long before colleagues had revived my sobriquet from college— the Ice Queen. Strangely, I didn't mind, as work was my identity. But my indifference to other people's perceptions changed once I left Arthur Andersen to begin my own firm."

Susan was awaiting sentencing as a result of her pleading guilty to criminal charges under Title 18 of the United States Code, Section 1519. That statute reads as follows:

> *Whoever knowingly alters, destroys, mutilates, conceals, covers up, falsifies, or makes a false entry in any record, document, or tangible object with the intent to impede, obstruct, or influence the investigation or proper administration of any matter with the jurisdiction of any department of agency of the United States...Shall be fined under this title, imprisoned not more than 20 years, or both.*

"The prosecutor wants to lock me in prison for years!" Susan clenched her jaw, then shook her head. "I can't get over how I allowed myself to stumble into this mess. It was like quicksand, just gradually pulling me in deeper and deeper. In a reckless attempt to please a client, my entire life's work has been ravaged."

"You talk about one client," I pointed out. "Was it only one?"

"Well, as a small business owner I needed to provide excellent service to all of my clients. But I had one client, Oliver, an art broker in Beverly Hills, and his business was important because he referred many others to me. His importance as a client to my firm clouded my judgment."

"What did Oliver ask of you?"

"I had been Oliver's accountant for 11 years, and I prepared his tax returns based on the records that he provided. My problems stemmed from his tax return for 2007."

"What kind of records did Oliver provide you to complete his tax return?"

"The standard records. I had his bank statements, check stubs, and checkbook sheets that recorded cash receipts and disbursements. Oliver and his wife regularly reported income from commissions he received on art sales. But the 2007 return included a sizeable income that I should've been more diligent in verifying."

"What happened in 2007," I asked. "Why was that year different?"

"When I received the records from Oliver for that year, they showed an income of $190,000 from commissions. I recorded the commissions on the Schedule C as self-employment income. But the checkbook sheet included a deposit entry for $1.3 million. It didn't show where the income came from. So I called Oliver and asked him how I should classify the deposit. He was evasive, reluctant to provide details, but when I told him that I needed to classify the income on the tax return Oliver told me that he had sold a painting from his collection. Getting information from him was like pulling teeth. If he hadn't referred so many clients to me, I would've dropped him years before."

Susan went on to say that over the years, she and Oliver had had numerous conversations about income classifications. He understood the difference between ordinary income from his self-employment, which was to be reported on the Schedule C of a federal income tax return, and income from capital gains, which was to be reported on the Schedule D.

"Oliver was well aware of the tax implications of short-term versus long-term capital gains. When I pressed him on how long he had owned the painting, he said that he had owned it for longer than one year, that I should classify the $1.3 million deposit as a long-term capital gain."

Five months after filing Oliver's 2007 tax return, two IRS agents approached Susan to discuss the tax documents. The agents were inquiring about Susan's telephone conversation with Oliver regarding the painting that he said he had sold from his collection. She told the agents that Oliver said he had owned the paintings for longer than one year, and that when she pressed him for a date of when he had acquired the painting, Oliver told her that he wasn't sure, but that she should use a date of just over a year before he sold it. The agents took notes, then served Susan with a subpoena to appear before a grand jury. When she appeared before the grand jury, a federal prosecutor questioned her about the telephone conversation she had with Oliver regarding the painting that he said he had sold from his collection for $1.3 million, and she testified truthfully in the same way that she had answered the IRS agents when they questioned her in her office.

Through the use of the grand jury, the prosecutor was investigating whether Oliver had filed a false tax return in violation of Title 26 of the Unites States Code, Section 7206. In addition to gathering testimony from Susan, the prosecutor called upon others who were involved with Oliver's transaction. That investigation uncovered Oliver's intricate deceit.

"Oliver never owned the painting at all." Susan told me. "As it turned out, he lied to me from the start and I was caught in the cover up."

"What do you mean," I asked.

"Maria was a client of Oliver's, and she owned a painting by Pablo Picasso that she asked Oliver to sell. Maria set an asking price of $4 million and agreed to pay Oliver a 10 percent commission if he sold the Picasso. Oliver than approached Jonathan, an affluent art buyer, and Jonathan agreed to buy the Picasso for $5.1 million. The commission apparently, wasn't enough for Oliver. So he deceived Maria by telling her that he had found a buyer who had offered $3.6 million for the Picasso; if she

135

accepted, Oliver said, Oliver said he would waive his commission. Maria agreed.

"With the sale cinched, Oliver instructed the buyer, Jonathan, to wire the $5.1 million to Oliver's escrow attorney. With the wire transfer complete, Oliver instructed the escrow attorney to deduct $10,000 as an escrow fee, and to remit the $3.6 million sales price to Maria. He also gave instructions for the escrow attorney to send payments totaling $180,000 to various others. Those additional payments didn't have any relationship to the sale of the Picasso, but by instructing his attorney to remit the payments from the escrow account, Oliver avoided the record of such funds passing through his own account. Finally, Oliver told his attorney to wire him the $1.3 million that remained from the sale of Maria's Picasso."

"It sounds like Oliver ripped off Maria for more than a million dollars." I said.

"Well he deceived her, but she agreed to sell the painting. I know Maria is pursuing a civil case against him for fraud. But Oliver dragged me into this mess by claiming that the income was a long-term capital gain rather than ordinary income."

"I don't understand how this became your problem," I said to Susan. "All you did was prepare a tax return that you based on the information Oliver provided. When the IRS agents questioned you, you answered truthfully. And you said that you testified truthfully to the grand jury. Why were you charged with a crime?"

"Like I said, the investigation into Oliver's taxes was ongoing long after I spoke with the IRS agents and after I testified in front of the grand jury. When I responded to the questions I didn't know the intricacies of Oliver's scheme or that the agents were looking into Schedule C versus Schedule D income on Oliver's tax return. I had taken Oliver at his word that he had sold a painting he had owned in his collection. Yet Oliver had lied to me, and when he learned that the IRS was investigating his tax return for the year 2007, he started changing his story and pressuring me to go along with him."

Susan told Oliver about the inquiry by the IRS and her grand jury appearance. He then began badgering her with questions about what she had been asked and precisely how she had answered. When Susan said that she had responded honestly, Oliver insisted that she accompany him to a meeting with his lawyer. Susan told me that she hadn't been enthusiastic about meeting with Oliver's lawyer, but because of Oliver's support for her practice over the years she felt obliged to help him. Before attending the meeting with Oliver and his lawyer, Susan drafted notes in which she again reiterated that Oliver had told her that he had sold a painting he had owned for longer than one year.

"While we were in front of the lawyer," Susan told me, "Oliver began denying that he had ever said he 'owned' the painting. Instead, he began insisting that what he said was that he 'had' the painting for longer than one year—not owned it. He was trying to lay the blame on me for misunderstanding him."

"Was a misunderstanding of what he said a possibility," I asked.

"Not a possibility." Susan held her hand up, as if showing me the stop sign. "If Oliver had not told me that he owned the painting, the length of time the Picasso was in his collection wouldn't have had any relevance. I knew that, Oliver knew that, and the lawyer knew that. Without his owning the painting, there wouldn't have been an issue of capital gains at all. The $1.3 million would have been ordinary self-employment income. I would have itemized it as a commission on the Schedule C of the tax return if Oliver hadn't told me he owned the painting for longer than one year. But the lawyer asked me the same questions you did—whether I could've misunderstood Oliver."

"And how did you answer the lawyer?"

"Well I should have put a stop to the charade right then and there," Susan said. "But at that moment I felt trapped. I don't even think that I answered. I just looked over at Oliver, shaking my head, silent, wondering how he could be asking me to lie. But while I was shaking my head no, Oliver was nodding his head yes, then saying that of course I misunderstood him."

At the time of Susan's meeting with Oliver and his lawyer, Susan didn't know anything about the Picasso transaction between Oliver and Maria, nor did she know about the shady way Oliver had instructed his attorney to disburse funds—and in so doing—concealing another $200,000 in ordinary income that Oliver didn't report.

As I listened to Susan describe her meeting with Oliver and his lawyer, I was painfully reminded of a similar meeting I once had with a hedge-fund manager, his client, and a team of the client's advisors. I was supposed to be overseeing the hedge fund, but in that moment I was put on the spot. Whereas Susan's pressure point was that she wanted to help a valued client, mine was in trying to protect a monthly income stream that the hedge fund was generating fraudulently. I told Susan about my experience, where it led me, and what I learned from it. Then I asked what she did in the meeting.

"The client's always right," Susan said. "It was against my better judgment and I regret what I did, but I went along with the plan by agreeing it was possible that I could've misunderstood Oliver. I felt dirty as soon as I said it, though that was only the start. As soon as I agreed that it was possible I could've misunderstood Oliver, the lawyer produced an affidavit for my signature."

"What did the affidavit say?"

"It was a frame up, attributing the misclassification of Oliver's profit to my own mistake and error. It went on to say that Oliver was in no way attempting to misrepresent the transaction concerning the painting and that the issue arose from nothing more than a miscommunication."

Susan told the lawyer she wasn't comfortable with the affidavit and suggested modifications that would make it more vague. Then Oliver ratcheted up the pressure by saying that based upon their longstanding relationship he didn't want to have to take legal action against Susan. She interpreted Oliver's words as a threat of a malpractice suit. As a compromise, Oliver's lawyer drafted a document releasing Susan from all liability for her role in preparing the 2007 tax return. With that signed release, Susan signed the affidavit for Oliver.

Susan then prepared and filed an amended tax return for Oliver. In the amended return, the $1.3 million was filed appropriately on the Schedule C as gross income rather than as a capital gain, and it included the additional tax payment that Oliver owed.

"But I take it that the amended return didn't resolve Oliver's problem," I said.

"Not only did it not resolve his problem, it created a massive problem for me." Susan folded her arms and leaned back in her chair. "Six months later, the IRS agents who initially interviewed me about Oliver returned to my office. They brought with them Oliver's original tax return, the amended tax return, the affidavit I signed, their notes from the previous time they questioned me, and transcripts from testimony that I gave to the grand jury. After pointing out the conflicting statements I gave about Oliver's supposed ownership of the Picasso and the income classification, they threatened me. They told me it was one crime to lie to federal officers. It was another crime to lie to a grand jury. It was another crime to obstruct a federal investigation. And it was another crime to fabricate records. Their aggression really shook me, humiliating me in my office."

Susan said that she tried to reason with the IRS agents, feebly claiming that she had simply signed the affidavit to relieve pressures of an angry client and that all she wanted to do was make the problem go away. But the agents were livid, as if she had offended them personally. They told her what their investigation had uncovered. Oliver had not only cheated the IRS with the fraudulent tax return, they said, he had also cheated Maria out of more than a million dollars by deceiving her, and he filed a second fraudulent tax return by not revealing the $200,000 in additional income he concealed by inappropriately instructing his attorney to disburse those funds from the escrow account.

"The agents accused me of being complicit in all of Oliver's crimes and told me that I would be going to prison for 20 years. I had to hire a criminal defense attorney. I pleaded guilty to one count of fabricating records to obstruct justice, but I still don't know what's going to happen to me. All of this for trying to help a client out of his own mess. It's been going on for a year now, ruining my practice and driving me out of my mind. I can't believe this happened. I can't believe it."

Susan may have been trying to please a valued client, but the pressure to do so resulted in the compromising of her morals. She wasn't as venal as I readily acknowledge I was in my former career as a stockbroker. She would not have considered abandoning her honesty and morality for a dollar amount. Rather, she was pressured during a heated meeting with a trusted client and his lawyer and not thinking about self-aggrandizement. Yet the law did not distinguish motivations for committing a crime. Whether a person accepted a kickback, participated in a fraud for financial gain, or as Susan had done, signed documents that would obstruct a federal investigation, disgrace and imprisonment could result.

As one who has experienced the criminal justice system and all of its ancillary consequences, I could help Susan prepare for the challenges ahead. I explained what she could anticipate as she approached sentencing, steps she could take to ease her adjustment to prison, and help her understand that complexities of supervised release. Yet the most valuable advice I could offer her—or anyone for that matter—was to live with the confidence that Neil Weinberg and other role models expressed to me. Such confidence could only come with a full commitment to living an honest life, with a commitment to never sell out morality or ethics.

Chapter Eleven Questions

1. How can a professional resolve a dilemma between a valued client's unethical demands and the professional's individual commitment to honesty?

2. In what ways can ambition threaten an individual's integrity?

3. Describe the relationship between ethics in business and ethics in one's personal life?

Chapter Twelve
Ryan's Accounting Fraud

During the nearly 400 days I served in prison, I recorded my daily activities. It was a strategy that helped to ensure I was always productive and working toward the goals that I had set. I could use the daily journal entries to measure progress and to analyze whether my actions were consistent with my commitment to lead a values-centered life.

We didn't have access to computers in prison, so I wrote everything out with blue Bic pens that I purchased from the commissary for 38 cents each. I sent my writings home every day and my mother, Tallie, typed them for me and posted the writings on a daily blog I kept at JustinPaperny.com.

When I was writing those entries, I hoped that my work would help others understand that regardless of what bad deeds a person had made in the past, individuals could always redirect their lives. At any time we could cease making decisions that led to disgrace and begin making decisions that would help us reconcile with law abiding society.

Upon my return to society I had opportunities to log onto my Web site and interact with people who found value in my writings from prison. Most of the visitors I received were encountering their own troubles with the criminal justice system. They suffered through months of hopelessness as they tried to make sense out of their tragic decisions that had taken them so far away from the lives they had aspired to lead.

People reached out to me for guidance because my postings on the Web showed a day-by-day record of growth through the adversity of confinement. They needed that assurance that they could create meaning in their lives again. By pleading guilty to felony charges, many of the people with whom I communicated through my Web site felt as if they had lost their identities. They looked in the mirror and did not recognize themselves. Depression darkened their lives, making it difficult to meet family and personal responsibilities, or even to climb out of bed. Ryan was in such a shape when he posted a message on my Web site during the wee hours of the morning.

"It's 2.17 in the morning and I've been reading your postings on the Web for the past four hours. I'm going to prison. I don't know for how long—maybe five years. I can't take it. I don't know how I'll survive. Please help me. I'm not cut out for this."

When I woke in the morning I responded to Ryan, completely identifying with his sense of loss. He had been the chief financial officer of a large retailer that was based in the Northeast, a publicly traded company that had been growing rapidly. Before joining the retailer, Ryan had been working on the accounting team at a large firm that audited the retailer in its infancy, when it operated seven stores. Alex, the retailer's president and chief operating officer had worked closely with Ryan. Impressed with Ryan's competence and work ethic, Alex offered Ryan an attractive compensation package that included stock options if he would come on board as the retailer's chief financial officer. Ryan accepted.

Six years after Ryan joined the retailer it had grown into a chain of 81 stores with combined revenues that exceeded $500 million; four years later the retailer had more than 300 stores in 30 states with combined gross revenues of $2.8 billion. Its growth did not come without problems and Ryan explained how pressures from the job grew in geometric proportions, like a giant snowball that eventually buried him under an avalanche.

"I can't believe how I let myself get trapped in this mess," Ryan and I spoke through my Web conferencing system, and I could see his distress. He was wearing a bathrobe over pajamas, and his face was unshaven despite it being afternoon in his time zone. "It all started with one bad decision. Once I crossed that line, there just wasn't any turning back."

It sounded like a cliché, but Ryan expressed sentiments that I experienced as I was passing through my own struggles with the criminal justice system, and sentiments that I heard from so many others who contacted me for consultations. Individuals may study through their university years with the best of intentions. They may earn positions of distinction and trust in their chosen careers. Yet if they allowed pressures to influence their good judgment, as Ryan and so many others discovered, it became easier to violate ethics, possibly even criminal laws.

I asked Ryan to describe the pressures that began his ethical slide. "The problems all began when I discovered a slide in our company's gross profit margin." Ryan recalled. "It wasn't much, just a percentage point or two. But we were growing extremely fast. We had numerous financial partners and analysts who followed our performance closely. At the time we were operating about 70 stores and our target gross profit margin ranged between 16 and 17 percent; I created financial reports that would monitor how we were doing and my boss and I would discuss our performance every Tuesday morning."

"Who was your boss," I asked. "The CEO?"

"I reported to Alex, our company's chief operating officer and president. He and I had worked closely together for years."

Ryan explained that he and Alex worked together to investigate the cause for the slight drop in gross profit margins. Every fraction of a percent counted because financial analysts would scrutinize the company's quarterly financial reports for institutional investors. If the analysts discovered the drop in gross profit margins, they could conclude that the company's rapid expansion was coming at the expense of effective management. Such a report, Ryan and Alex understood, would bring unwanted selling pressure on the stock, thereby lowering the market capitalization, possibly lowering the company's credit rating and raising the costs creditors would demand for the company's debt. Both Ryan and Alex were determined to avoid the downward spiral by discovering the cause of the sinking gross profit margins.

"Our initial investigation revealed that one of our company's major suppliers was shipping less merchandise than it was billing our company to pay. Armed with the data from our investigation, Alex confronted our suppliers. He negotiated a seven-figure financial settlement. Once those funds were credited to our account, and our suppliers implemented systems to ensure the improper billing patterns would not persist, Alex and I celebrated, congratulating ourselves on solving the problem."

"And," I asked. "What happened?"

"All we did was put a bandage over the problem," Ryan said. "We didn't solve it."

Ryan explained that despite Alex's successful negotiations for a financial settlement with the retailer's suppliers, weekly financial reports that Ryan prepared showed that the gross profit margins continued to fall below expectations by at least one percentage point.

"When Alex and I reviewed the disappointing results, he instructed me to keep quiet about them. He didn't want me to reveal the reports to either the CEO or the board despite my obligations. Doing so would have raised awkward questions about Alex's performance as the company's chief operating officer. That was the moment our deceit began. Alex took it upon himself to alter the financial records so that the gross margins would match the historically expected margins. The scheme understated losses and reflected nonexistent profits."

"But if you were the CFO," I asked, "how could Alex alter the financial reports? Did he understand the accounting system so thoroughly?"

"It was simply a matter of manipulating spreadsheets," Ryan explained. "Alex understood our accounting system completely. He was the CFO before I came on board and he had put the original accounting system in place. We began working closely together when I was an auditor for the company's outside accountants and our history made me feel an allegiance to him. At first I was hesitant to participate, but since Alex began the initial alterations, and since he was my superior, I just shrugged and went along with it."

"I understood the pressure," I said, "but you had to know the complications that first decision could bring. Once Alex started to manipulate the numbers, how could you ever expect to balance them again? I mean, this wasn't a small enterprise. You guys had hundreds of millions in revenue. How could you juggle those numbers and still know where you really stood, or stay in control?"

"Well Alex started the manipulation of records, but I was sitting right beside him the whole time. He just started inserting the percentages we wanted in the appropriate columns, and we both understood the implications. We generated two sets of financial reports, and that became our regular pattern. One set of reports contained the false, altered numbers and the other set contained the real numbers. We tallied the difference between the real and falsified figures in a separate account that we called the sub-ledger. It became routine, week after week."

Ryan told me that the falsified reports understated liabilities and overstated earnings. The sub-ledger, meanwhile, contained net losses and remained secret between Ryan and Alex. The only financial reports the team distributed were the false reports, which they identified as "the board" reports.

But Ryan and Alex understood that it wasn't only the company's board of directors and chief executive officer that would rely upon the falsified financial reports. Every quarter, the Securities and Exchange Commission would require the company to file financial reports that all investors could review. As the company's chief financial officer, Ryan had an obligation to sign the reports, authenticating that the SEC financial filings accurately reflected the financial status of the company.

Title 18 of the United States Code, Section 1350, attached severe criminal penalties to corporate officers who filed false financial reports with the SEC. Ryan said that he understood those penalties could include fines of up to $5 million and 20 years imprisonment for each report that falsely represented the company's financial status to the SEC and investors.

"I understood the rules of strict compliance with Sarbanes-Oxley." Ryan identified the legislation that subjected him to criminal sanctions. "The funny thing was, once Alex and I started, we deluded ourselves into thinking that we were pulling off something spectacular. We got caught up in the excitement of creating a ploy that supposedly outfoxed everyone else. Neither of us considered the possibility of getting caught. We were getting away with it week after week, month after month, just digging ourselves into a deeper and deeper mess without even realizing it."

When making presentations to the company's lenders and investors, the chief executive officer unknowingly relied upon falsified financial reports that Ryan and Alex created. Those reports led a consortium of banks to increase credit lines by more than $150 million; they convinced private equity groups to purchase more than $300 million worth of the company's stock; they served as the basis to persuade investment houses to infuse the retailer with more than $100 million in exchange for 10-years secured notes that the company issued. All of that liquidity contributed to the company's massive expansion and inflated the price of the stock under false pretenses. What began as an effort to conceal a decline of gross profit margins escalated into a fraud of massive proportions that ultimately victimized thousands of individual investors.

"But how did you keep the fraud going for so long?" It seemed to me that with so many professional investors involved, someone would have discovered it. "Didn't the false numbers eventually stand out like a bright light?"

"The numbers didn't stand out because we offset them."

"With what?"

"With exclusivity funds." Ryan explained that Alex had negotiated with several vendors who agreed to make large payments to the retailer in exchange for exclusive rights to supply the retailer's growing number of stores with particular types of merchandise. "During the first year we were able to offset all of the losses in the sub ledger with these funds."

"Weren't you supposed to records those exclusivity funds as income?"

Ryan answered my question by explaining that, according to generally accepted accounting principles, the exclusivity payments should have been amortized over the term of the contract. The retailer should have recognized a portion of the income each year and accounted for the balance as a liability that the retailer would have to repay if it broke the contract.

"We circumvented the accounting problem in the same way we got around the other problems—by manipulating the financial spreadsheets and reports to suit our needs. Income from the exclusivity deals was like a slush fund with millions that we used to conceal the fraud. That money bailed us out of one problem but it created another. Both Alex and I knew we had crossed the point of no return."

That sub-ledger and the exclusivity funds enabled both Ryan and Alex to hide other inappropriate personal benefits. They diverted corporate funds for personal use, to pay for such costs as home improvements, jewelry, vacations, and automobiles. What's more, neither Ryan nor Alex declared those embezzled funds as income on their personal tax filings; such omissions exposed each to felony charges of tax evasion, in violation of Title 26 of the United States Code, Sanction 7206.

"How could that happen?" I scratched my head, puzzled on the thought that no one in the accounting department would have discovered such a diversion of funds. "You're telling me that the company could disperse checks to contractors, jewelry stores, hotels, and car dealerships? Wouldn't someone have noticed?"

"If we would have made the disbursements through appropriate channels someone may have noticed and raised questions. But we concealed them." Ryan described how he used a standard typewriter to write the checks instead of processing them through the computer system. By using the typewriter he could avoid detection from others who worked in the accounting department and he could prevent leaving a trail for auditors. He manipulated corporate ledgers with falsified receivables to offset expenses and make accounts appear to balance.

"Didn't the accountants who audited the business's operations become suspicious with all of the discrepancies?" The size of the fraud that Ryan and Alex were juggling seemed too large to manage for a period of years without detection.

Ryan told me that, on average, the retailer was adding one new store to the chain each week, bringing the total number of stores to well over 100 when the fraud was in full operation. Although the sub-ledger he created with Alex concealed more than $40 million in corporate losses and inappropriate expenditures, he kept auditors from discovering the fraud by inflating inventory levels in stores that he knew the auditors would not visit.

The elaborate, calculated scheming that Ryan described contradicted assertions he made about not setting out to ruin his life by engaging in fraud. He had earned his accounting degree and his MBA at New York University. While there, he said that be participated in the requisite ethics courses.

"I aced my way through NYU, "he said, "and I always thought of myself as an honest, ethical person." Before he accepted the CFO position his career required continuing education, including ethics evaluations. "Every performance review I received at the accounting firm showed me to have the highest ethical standards when it came to ethics."

Obviously, Ryan lessened his allegiance to those high standards when he fell under the influence of Alex, his direct superior and chief executive officer who hired him. He described the moment of his initial slide.

"When I brought the weekly financial report to Alex, and it showed that the gross profit margins continued to disappoint, I wasn't considering fraud as a potential solution. But Alex looked at me, scraped his fingers through his hair and shook his head. Then he pulled the spreadsheet up on his computer, and when he saved it under a different name—as the board report—I had an inkling of what he was thinking. Then he clicked a few keys, changing percentages that would manipulate the totals. He made a comment about how easy it could be to fix the problem. Instead of objecting right then, I simply went along, not fully seeing how far we would take it."

I probed in order to understand more about the underlying reasons for Ryan's decisions. After listening to my questions, he leaned back in his chair and thought for a while in silence. As he shook his head, rubbed the back of his hand over the whiskers on his chin, I could see the humiliation. His explanation of wanting to conceal disappointing profit margins and support his boss didn't seem sufficient reason to actively participate in fraud.

"Deep inside," he finally said, "I suppose I was concerned about the value of stock options I had. They represented a significant portion of my net worth, but they were still under restriction, prohibiting me from cashing out for another six months. If I hadn't agreed, I knew that Alex and I would have had no choice but to disclose the disappointing numbers. We may have lost our jobs, but the real pain would have been the market. Institutional investors would have dumped the stock, decimating the value of my positions. I just never thought it would get so out of hand. Once we started, we couldn't turn back without exposing the crime."

The crime, as Ryan came to acknowledge, began to torment him more when the fraud reached out into the stratosphere. He feared arrest, imprisonment, humiliation. He sought psychological counseling, took antidepressant medications. When the losses exceeded $50 million he couldn't cope with the anxiety further and voluntarily exposed the fraud to the United States Attorney's Office.

"How did federal prosecutors respond to your confession?"

"There were three, and they listened to me for four hours," Ryan said, "with a stenographer and a tape recorder. Despite their repeated requests of whether I wanted an attorney, I declined. I just needed to get it all off my chest. The guilt was crushing me, suffocating me. I had to let the chips fall. At that point I didn't care what happened. I wanted to cleanse myself."

"Did you eventually retain an attorney?"

"Oh yes, and when I did, he scolded me for saying anything without consulting an attorney first. But in the end, I think, I did the right thing—the best I could do."

The prosecutors told Ryan that—based on his confession and all the schemes he participated in—the government could charge him with numerous crimes. One included Interstate Transportation of Property Obtained by theft or fraud, codified at Title 18 of the United States Code, Section 2314. It provides that:

> *Whoever transports, transmits, or transfers in interstate or foreign commerce any goods, wares, merchandise, securities or money, of the value of $5,000 or more, knowing the same to have been stolen, converted, or taken by*

fraud...Shall be fined under this title or imprisoned not more than ten years, or both....

For every unauthorized check that Ryan caused to be issued, prosecutors said he could face a separate criminal count. He also faced numerous charges including mail fraud, wire fraud, bank fraud, securities fraud, and filing false income tax returns.

"When the prosecutors finally finished reciting all the charges I faced, I thought they might be burying me under the prison. But my full cooperation helped. Because of my confession and my exposing the crimes voluntarily, the government agreed to charge me with a single count of fraud that would expose me to a maximum of five years. I know it could've been worse, but I don't even think I'll be able to handle what's coming."

Chapter Twelve Questions

1. What purpose does the Sarbanes Oxley legislation that Ryan described serve?

2. In what ways does accounting fraud influence the public markets?

3. Who bears responsibility when investors base sales or purchase decisions on falsified financial reports?

Chapter Thirteen
Peter's Good Intentions

When I spoke with audiences about taking steps to cultivate habits that lead to good character I always invited questions. Understandably, people frequently told me during those exchanges that they considered themselves ethical people and that they couldn't envision a scenario that would lead them to cross ethical lines. When I heard such assertions I applauded their level of certainty, the strong moral compass expressed. Then to lighten the mood, I offered a joke I heard while I was in prison.

An older man with a prosperous look about him sat at a bar. After eyeing a striking young woman, he approached her. Wasting little time with small talk, the man propositioned her. "If I were to give you $5 million would you sleep with me?"

The woman paused for a moment while looking at the man, surprised at the question. When she answered, she said yes.

"Would you sleep with me for $50?" the man followed up.

"What do you think I am? A prostitute?"

"We've already established that," the man said. "Now we're simply negotiating on the price."

The point I strove to make in telling the joke was that failing to practice habits of good character leaves us vulnerable to falling off track. A strong moral center could provide a foundation. Yet my observations convinced me that the foundation, or self-perception, wouldn't significantly protect us from the possibility of falling of course. To paraphrase the wisdom of Gandhi, we had to ensure that everything we thought, everything we said, and everything we did stayed in harmony with our strong moral center. When we made such practices part of our daily lives—like brushing our teeth—we wouldn't even consider propositions or actions that were inconsistent with the honest, trustworthy people we considered ourselves to be.

News reports made clear to me, however, that many among us crossed ethical lines, and even broke criminal laws, while still considering themselves as morally upstanding citizens. In February 2010, for example, *Time* magazine reported that 95 percent of all digital music was downloaded illegally. Artists and industry executives considered such piracy as theft, no different from stealing a record off the shelf of a music store. Musicians and those who sponsored their work had a massive investment in time and money to make products available to consumers, yet it was clear that many of those consumers did not consider ethical implications—or criminality—when pirating music by downloading it illegally.

While in prison I met many people who considered themselves ethical, trustworthy, and honest. They were men who grew up in stable communities, men who lived with aspirations of leadership and saw themselves as good citizens. They never envisioned possibilities that could lead them into struggles with the criminal justice system. Circumstances surfaced, however, that took them off course. Despite self-perceptions of having strong moral centers, their lack of focus on making values-based decisions and leading harmonious lives, blinded their judgment.

Chapter Thirteen

Peter was an example of just such a man. He was in his early 40s when we met at a Starbucks near my home. He sat alone at a table, his Bible and other religious books open in front of him as I walked in. With gold-framed glasses, sandy hair that he kept cut short, posture that suggested decades of sedentary work, and soft hands more accustomed to gripping pens or telephone handsets than picks or shovels, Peter personified management of small business. Curious about what would bring such a man into trouble with the law, I introduced myself and thanked him for contacting me. Peter called me on recommendation from his attorney.

Peter's identity, as it turned out, was rooted in his Mormon faith. He described himself as being of "pioneer heritage," meaning that he took family pride in that his ancestors had been part of the settlers who crossed America with Brigham Young and the founders of the Mormon Church. Peter was one of six children of loving parents, both of whom had careers as schoolteachers in the city of Liberty, Utah. The devout family was active in church participation.

Peter told me that character and veracity had been of the highest importance to him since he was a young child. "I can still remember the first lie I told," he said, "and the shame that tormented my conscience for years afterwards."

"What was it?" I asked.

He laughed. "It's funny to think back on it. I was in the sixth grade in band class. We had a teacher who was kind of strict. I had to use the bathroom, but I was nervous about asking permission so I tried to hold it, squeezing my legs together to block the urge. When the time was right I dashed off to the bathroom, but I didn't make it. I wet my pants and the stain embarrassed me. My best friend asked me what happened. Being too embarrassed to admit that I'd

158

wet my pants, I lied, telling him that I had fallen in a puddle. I was so bothered by the way I felt about myself after telling the lie, that I vowed I would never lie again."

As I listened to Peter tell me how being honest became integral to his life at such a young age, and about his devotion to the Mormon faith, I wondered what would have prompted him into affairs that led to his troubles with the law. He told me that he had graduated high school in 1987, and after a two-year mission "to proselytize, to teach, and to baptize," Peter finished studies at Weber State University and graduated with a degree in technical sales.

While describing his background, Peter said that when he was 23 he married Shauna, who also studied at Weber State and was active with him in Mormon Church groups. The couple supported themselves by managing apartment buildings and through Peter's earnings as a sales representative for an electronics company. Peter's ambition, however, was to establish himself in a business of his own. He considered himself an entrepreneur at heart and aspired to both the freedom of time and the profits that would come with business ownership. He and Shauna welcomed the first of four children into their family in 1994, and in 1995, when he was 26, Peter launched his first business.

Attending church services regularly, Peter was observant of the necktie styles many of the young men wore on Sundays. Some of the young men in his church wore ties with prints of cartoon characters. Being a devout Mormon, Peter didn't think such attire was appropriately reverent for church services, and his judgment on neckties sparked an idea. Despite having no experience in the apparel industry, Peter began to make some inquiries.

Research convinced Peter that an apparel company in the Orient could manufacture and deliver ties featuring his own design at a net cost of $2 per tie. Since neckties typically sold at prices of $20 each in his area, Peter believed he could persuade local retailers to purchase the ties from him at a fair wholesale price that would provide a sufficient mark-up. Using his personal computer, Peter designed neckties in solid colors with small images of a Mormon temple. He formed a company that he called "Temple Ties" and soon took delivery of 1,200 neckties.

Without advance purchase orders from established retailers, Peter had to create his own distribution system. He presented his ties to local businesses, offering to sell them on consignment. Temple Ties became a success, giving Peter a sense of accomplishment.

To meet the growing demand for neckties and other products Temple Ties offered, Peter needed additional capital. He brought in a financial partner and over the next two years the business thrived. Peter's business naiveté along with his tendency to trust, however, made him susceptible to manipulation. His partner swindled him, he said, forcing him to walk away from Temple Ties three years after starting the company in his living room.

Having successfully launched one small business, Peter couldn't bring himself to return to the workplace as someone else's employee. Even though his wily partner at Temple Ties had taken advantage of his trust, Peter appreciated the learning experience and he realized that he enjoyed the adrenaline rush that came with the pressure of running his own company. He became obsessed with starting a new business venture.

That obsession with business led Peter to neglect other areas of his life. He described himself as a workaholic who—while searching frantically for the next big opportunity—gave insufficient attention to his duties as a husband and father. While his wife wanted Peter to participate in family responsibilities and restore stability, Peter yearned for the money and freedom that came with the success he'd achieved with Temple Ties. As Peter cocooned himself in his home office contemplating new business ideas, the family's financial resources ran dry. That loss of balance weakened Peter and his marriage began to suffer.

He launched a second apparel company that failed. Then he tried other importing ideas without success. Months without generating income turned into years, leading to dampened spirits and diminished energy levels. Peter was desperate, and when a man pitched him on the idea that riches could be made by mining gold from a Mexican mountain, Peter became intrigued. Despite his lack of experience or knowledge of mining, he devoted six months to raising $200 thousand in capital from investors to further the gold mining effort, but in the end the venture yielded only dirt—albeit of high Mexican quality, but it was still just dirt.

By 2005, the bank holding his mortgage had foreclosed on his family's home and Peter's wife divorced him. Sad and broken, Peter said he was eager for any type of income-generating opportunity to win back his wife's respect and love. It was in that state of mind that Peter agreed to join the business that led to his problems with the law: property management.

Gordon, an acquaintance of Peter's, explained how his experience with Internet data mining allowed him to scan public records in search of single-family homes that banks were about to foreclose upon. Gordon suggested that Peter approach the homeowners to offer property management services. After listening to Gordon's idea, Peter agreed.

Peter would contact the homeowners who were about to lose their properties to foreclosure. If the homeowners would move out and vacate the property, Peter said that he would work toward the possibility of arranging a short sale. (A short sale meant a sale of the property for an amount less than what was owed on the mortgage.) The short sale would not cause as much damage as a foreclosure would to the homeowner's credit score. If the homeowners agreed to vacate the property, Gordon paid Peter a commission, then Gordon would rent the property out, keeping the income generated by the rental until the bank either foreclosed or agreed to a short sale.

Peter said he did not question the legality of such a venture. Since he had lost his home to foreclosure, he knew the process was gut-wrenching. By convincing the homeowners to vacate early, he convinced himself that he was providing a service that would spare the family some humiliation and give them an opportunity to put themselves back on track. With a short sale on their credit report rather than a foreclosure, Peter told the families that they would not face as much resistance when they attempted to purchase another house.

He saw his service as a way of helping the families make a new start, and the entrepreneurial aspects of property management enticed him. He could establish his own hours, and the income he earned would allow him to show his ex-wife that he was becoming more stable. During his first year in property management, Peter earned $60 thousand enabling him to pay his child-support obligations. Rather than expressing admiration, Peter's ex-wife questioned the legitimacy of his venture.

"How can you collect rental payments from a property you don't own?" Shauna asked with skepticism.

"I'm not collecting the rent," Peter countered. "I'm being paid to persuade the homeowners to vacate the property early so I can work to arrange a short sale before the banks foreclose."

"But your so-called partner collects rent on properties that he doesn't have any rights to, and you're helping him. How can you say that's legal?"

"Well, it is."

Shauna's persistent questions shook Peter's confidence. During his second year of property management, he consulted an attorney for clarification. The attorney explained that Peter was involved in a risky venture that potentially could expose him to a variety of criminal charges. Only adherence to strict boundaries (that included full disclosure to apprise lenders and possible bankruptcy trustees of rental income from the properties) would keep Peter within the law. After talking with the lawyer, Peter realized that all of his practices didn't comply, but he was on track to earn $90,000 that year. So long as he was honest with the homeowners, Peter convinced himself that the business could continue.

Peter's delusion came to an end early one morning when eight federal officers wearing bulletproof vests woke him with their weapons drawn and pointed at him. They searched his records, questioned him, and confiscated his computer in their quest to gather evidence. Over the next four years the authorities disrupted his life while building a criminal case against him. In time, the man who said that he considered himself moral, ethical, and honest pleaded guilty to criminal charges of fraud, in violation of the United States Criminal Code, Title 18, which makes participating in swindles a federal crime. Peter was sentenced to serve 24 months and was burdened with a criminal restitution order of $300,000, which will hamper his life after prison.

When Peter told me his story, he was looking for guidance on how to make the most of his prison term. I empathized with his tendency to deny that he had crossed criminal lines, as I had once comforted myself with the same kinds of denials. What I had more trouble grasping was his apparent willingness to continue with the property management charade after his conscience convinced him it could be wrong, and especially after a lawyer confirmed that his actions violated criminal laws. It was disturbing to see the regularity with which people refused to accept how violating clearly written criminal codes belied their assertions of personal commitments to morality, to virtue, and to honesty.

On 21 January 2010, for example, Diona B. Henriques published a front-page story in *The New York Times*. The title screamed "F.B.I Sting Snares Arms Sellers; Bribes for Foreign Deals Charged." The article described an undercover Justice Department operation to prosecute people who violated the Foreign Corrupt Practices Act. That law prohibits American citizens and companies from bribing foreign government officials for business purpose. Despite the clarity of the anti-bribery law, 22 top-level business executives sent written confirmation that they would pay bribes and that they participated in individual "test" deals the federal agents contrived. Reminding me of Peter, the story described one executive who consulted with an outside law firm to inquire about his vulnerability to criminal prosecution. Despite legal advice from counsel to reject the corrupt proposal, the executive attempted to subvert the law to close the deal.

Without question, those business executives considered themselves honest, ethical people. My guess was that given the opportunity to answer simple questions of whether they understood the difference between right and wrong, as Peter did and as I once did, those business executives would have answered that they could distinguish right from wrong. Not one of those executives could have imagined on the morning of 19 February 2010 that he would be arrested by Federal agents at gunpoint and taken away in handcuffs while industry colleagues at a trade show looked on.

At what point did those people who considered themselves honest and ethical become vulnerable to crossing lines that would expose them to the criminal justice system? They were well educated; they were serving the corporate community in positions of responsibility; and they presumably understood laws that prohibited corrupt practices. Nevertheless, despite written codes, an understanding of right and wrong, and legal counsel, the prospect of millions of dollars worth of corrupt business compelled them to cross lines that resulted in their being charged with violating criminal laws. Besides charges of corruption, the executives faced money laundering charges that carried prison terms of 20 years.

The more I listened to people like Peter, and the more stories my research revealed about people like the business executives ensnared in the sting operation, the more convinced I became that regardless of how moral or ethical an individual perceived himself today, without the daily cultivation of good character, anyone could fall off track. This was a lesson that students and business executives alike would be well advised to embrace. As Lanny Breuer, the United States assistant attorney general said, "We are going to bring all the innovations of our organized crime and drug war cases to the fight against white-collar crime."

Peter told me that he had grown up with a commitment to honesty. When people in audiences I addressed told me that they were honest, ethical people, and that they couldn't envision scenarios that would lead them to cross ethical lines, I sometimes thought of Peter. He had said that even thoughts of dishonesty brought back uncomfortable memories from childhood of wetting his pants. Yet he was on his way to serving a 24-month sentence in federal prison. Peter hoped to redeem his good character, but his story made clear that no one was immune from the need to train and exercise a commitment to ethics. Unfortunately, as *Time* magazine reported in its story about illegal digital downloads of music, millions of people who presumably identified themselves as being honest regularly engaged in theft.

Chapter Thirteen Questions

1. What did Peter's self-description about being a workaholic imply about his values?

2. How did Peter's definition of success influence his ability to make ethical decisions?

3. How do commitments to make ethical decisions compare to commitments to comply with the law?

Chapter Fourteen
Jason's View on Caveat Emptor

The Spanish-American philosopher George Santayana wrote that those who didn't understand history were doomed to repeat it. Santayana taught the kinds of abstract lessons that I should have paid more attention to learning and comprehending when I studied at USC. I didn't. Rather than truly learning valuable lessons from history and the life experiences of others, I memorized what I had to know to satisfy requirements for each course and moved on. For that myopia, and the bad judgment that followed, I continue to pay a price.

Consistent with Santayana's written wisdom, the missed opportunities to learn from others doomed me to repeat history—and to suffer through the lasting consequences. My complicity in securities fraud took place in 2004. Yet it wasn't until 2008 that my judicial proceedings concluded, and it wasn't until 2009 that I walked out of prison. Leaving prison, however, would not conclude the enduring sting of the criminal justice system. Like Sisyphus rolling the boulder up the hill of Hades, only to have the rock roll down again, I would carry the burden of my conviction for a lifetime.

I was not the first person to succumb to temptations of greed and self-interest. Many people lived with similar weaknesses, but the choices others made would not excuse my disregard for the values of good character that should have guided my decisions. Biblical writings, philosophers, and news reports provided infinite lessons I could have learned from. Despite such examples, I never envisioned the consequences for bad decisions that ensnared others as having any relationship to the privileged life I led. Many white-collar offenders I've since met expressed that same willful ignorance. As Shakespeare wrote some 400 years ago, it was a tangled web that we all wove.

My criminal action may have occurred in 2004, and my prison term may have ended in 2009, but I'm still caught in the web of my deceit. We live in a world where the decisions of our past—especially the bad decisions—stay with us. A Google search yields information about us that we're incapable of burying. I'm constantly chagrined by my past. When I meet new people and they ask what I do, I won't permit myself to hide through half-truths or lies. Instead, I brace myself for a new blow to my sense of self as I reveal my history of imprisonment and describe how I try to teach others what I learned from it; the blow may come with a look of shock, surprise, or disgust rather than a slap across the face, but the sting still feels the same.

I did not consider my gradual disregard for the importance of ethics as a conscience choice. It just happened. Despite ample evidence that was available through history and the consequences that others experienced, I couldn't imagine my ethical slide leading to criminal actions. Since I couldn't conceive of myself as a "criminal," I certainly couldn't envision the infinite numbers of collateral consequences that would accompany a felony conviction. Those were burdens that I mistakenly thought applied to others—not me.

When I returned to society after imprisonment I was in my mid-30s, eager to resume life as I had known it before my bad decisions created my mess. I quickly

169

learned, however, that although I could learn to live with the stigma of my felony, I could never outrun it. Like a dark shadow, the felony always covered me. I'd meet a woman that I hoped to build a relationship with, and then the awkward moment would come when I'd have to reveal my criminal history, forcing her to carry the awkward burden as well. The humiliation would never end.

Besides imprisonment, my sanction required that I prostrate myself to a probation officer. I'd have to confer with him regularly, to seek his permission to travel outside of the Los Angeles area. I could not even disburse my resources in a manner that I saw fit without consulting him first. During my year away I incurred numerous expenses that only increased when I returned to society. When I received a windfall in the form of an income tax refund I hoped to pay off my debt. But I couldn't make the decision on my own. Instead, I had an obligation to apprise my probation officer. We had a cordial relationship and when I told him of the unexpected check I received he applauded my honesty. Then he told me in no uncertain terms that he would take me back to court if I did not immediately surrender the entire check as a partial payment toward my six-figure restitution order.

Although resources were available for me to understand the consequences of an inattention to ethics, I choose to ignore them. Because of that choice I am doomed to live with the scarlet letter and ancillary effects that come with my felony conviction. I blame only myself for not paying more attention to the wisdom of history, or of learning more from others. And I don't find any consolation in speaking with other white-collar offenders who tell me about unexpected troubles that eviscerated their lives because of their own disregard for ethical standards.

"I just never thought my decisions would come back to bite me like this," Jason said. He sat across from me at a Starbucks in Santa Monica, hair disheveled, his coffee shaking in his hand. Lines etched his face and I noticed that he had missed several spots when shaving. Personal appearance lost relevance when fortunes reversed. "Now I'm not only a convicted felon, I'm also losing all of my assets through bankruptcy, my wife and I are both going to prison, and our two children will have to move to Arizona to live with their grandparents while my wife and I serve our sentences."

"Why didn't your wife come with you today," I asked. "Don't you think learning about the system she's going into would have helped her as well?"

"She won't even talk to me," Jason reached for his handkerchief, removed his glasses and dabbed his eyes. "We're sleeping in separate rooms. We've been together since college, 12 years and we built our business together, as a team, but she blames me for everything."

"What's her name?"

"Cindy. She's an accountant, or I should say she was an accountant. Her lawyer said that the felony conviction would result in the loss of her license. We're both going to have to start from scratch when our prison terms end. If we serve the entire seven years, we'll be in our 40s, without any assets. I don't know whether our marriage is going to survive the separation and disruption. I don't know what will become of our children."

"Although I've never been married, and I don't have any children, I know what it's like to lose everything." I always empathize when I meet offenders who struggle with the criminal justice system. They frequently feel alone, desperate, and hopeless. I know that an understanding ear can help. "I lost my licenses to sell securities and real estate. My own uncle disowned me—he says that my felony conviction disgraced the family and that I deserve whatever comes to me. But you know what?

Despite the difficulties, I've learned many lessons from the experience—lessons that I should've learned before. It's never too late. On account of what I've learned, I know that my life gets better every day. Because of the lessons, when I do find a wife, I will be a better husband, and when I do have children, I'll be a better father."

"That's probably easy to say now. Your prison term is behind you. My wife and I haven't even started to serve ours, and if nothing changes, we'll have to stay in there for seven years. That's a lifetime. Our kids will be in high school. How can we keep our family bonds strong with this kind of stress? We shouldn't even be going through this."

"Seven years is a long sentence, I know, about seven times longer than what I served. And I don't say this to diminish the challenges ahead, but as I did when I was inside, you're going to meet people who have served much longer terms. You'll also meet people who have served much shorter terms. What's going to surprise you, I think, is that the real challenge isn't the length of your sentence—but whether you create meaning from it."

Jason stared blankly. "What's that?" He leaned back in the booth. "I don't follow."

"You've got choices to make. The perspective you and your wife choose will determine how both of you emerge. If the only view you allow yourself is all of the losses that you've suffered, I worry that only misery will accompany you on the road ahead. For prisoners who cling to such negative views, every day feels like a month. Those who choose to learn from their experience, from the experience of others who've overcome the struggles of their own lives, they seem to work through much more positive adjustments. It's a lesson I learned, and a lesson that I hope both you and your wife will consider."

"How do you expect us to think about learning or meaning at a time like this?" Jason waved his hand away. "The government is tearing our family apart. The bankruptcy trustee will auction off our home. Our children's lives are being uprooted. In a matter of weeks both Cindy and I will surrender to prisons—we don't even know where. These aren't hypotheticals. I don't see how we have too many choices to make. The courts and government prosecutors have chosen everything for us."

"The danger, Jason, is that you don't recognize your perceptions as the greatest threat to your possibility for a positive adjustment. And although it may be difficult for you to perceive at this moment—when your entire world seems to be imploding—a negative adjustment would only bring greater instability to you and to your family."

"It is what it is," Jason told me. "I don't see how I can look at what's happening any differently. My family and I have lost everything."

"You haven't lost everything."

"What do you mean?" He removed his glasses, wiped both the lenses with his napkin, then set them on the table between us.

"You still have your life, and you have the choice of what you will make of it going forward."

"Well, that's kind of obvious. Isn't it?"

"I don't think so," I said. "At least it wasn't for me before my experience with the prison system."

He shook his head in disbelief. "So what are you saying, prison was good for you?"

"Tell me what you think," I said. "When I graduated from college I thought I had the golden ticket. Within a few months I was a stockbroker overseeing millions. But the pursuit of money drove me, influencing what I became as a person. Instead of living a life of honor and respectability, the choices I made conditioned me to lie and cheat. I would say and do anything to clinch a deal. My life didn't have direction, or at least I didn't pay attention to the signs. Wherever I looked, I saw men who were 25 years older than I was. They were unhealthy, on third and fourth marriages, and they had bad relationships with their children. Those who had a home couldn't make it there after work without first stopping for a few drinks. I should've been learning from all the unhappiness and unfilled lives around me. Instead, I was following down the same path. I gained weight, I couldn't nurture a relationship because I was too obsessed with work, I hurt the people that I loved. Those decisions—of leading a directionless life—led to my imprisonment, and it was there where I realized I had to make some changes. How about you? What kind of life have you been leading for the last 10 years?"

"Not much different, I suppose." Jason spoke more softly, as if sinking, breaking. "I've been drinking a lot. My wife and I don't get along as well as we should. Responsibilities at work have too frequently trumped my responsibilities as a father and husband. Part of the problem, I think, has been that Cindy and I work together. Our life has become all business."

"Didn't you say you were in the mortgage business?"

"We started out as mortgage brokers. That led us into the real estate business, and about five years ago we opened up a warehouse line and became mortgage bankers."

"Sounds pretty well integrated, enabling you to earn fees and commissions at every stage of the transaction."

"We had a good run until the market collapsed." Jason became more confident when he spoke about the business he built.

"Did you really?" I asked.

"What do you mean?"

"Have a good run, as you said. I mean, look where it got you."

"I meant we had a good run as far as the numbers we were posting."

"But what good were those numbers if pursuing them caused use to lose everything you set out to build, and your freedom besides?"

"Well, if the financial markets hadn't crashed, I wouldn't be in this mess."

"I thought you and your wife pleaded guilty to numerous counts of wire fraud and mail fraud?"

"We pleaded guilty because if we were to take the case to trial, our attorneys told us we could face sentences of 20 years or more. We just couldn't take that chance."

"But were you guilty? Did you commit mail fraud and wire fraud?"

Jason shrugged his shoulders. "I was a businessman. I didn't even know what those terms meant. As far as I was concerned, we were taking advantage of opportunities to put people into homes. That was it. The government accused us of fraud because too many of our customers defaulted and went into foreclosure."

Some of the offices that Jason and his wife operated, he told me, specialized in servicing people with poor credit ratings. Government prosecutors accused the husband-and-wife team of creating a business culture that rewarded agents and brokers to make real estate sales and issue mortgages to people they knew would default. Over a period of two years, more than 70 percent of the mortgage loans Jason's company issued—and then sold to the secondary market—went into default, resulting in losses exceeding $20 million. Prosecutors cited his firm as an example of "predatory lenders," who fraudulently coaxed unqualified and unsophisticated customers into purchases they didn't understand and couldn't afford.

"When I was a stockbroker," I told Jason, "I made numerous decisions that I knew were unethical. My only concern was generating higher commissions. It doesn't sound like the decisions you were making differed much. Am I reading you right?"

"That was the market," he shrugged again. "We were just dealing with the hand we had, doing what was necessary to compete. If I didn't serve those customers, one of my competitors was going to take the business."

I told Jason that what I came to acknowledge about my decisions was that they were dishonest, deceitful. People were hurt because of choices I made. I wasn't an honest stockbroker. My lack of professional integrity brought higher commissions for a while, but then the disaster followed, and not only for me. The choices I made caused pain for those who loved me, and for those whose trust was misplaced in me.

"How about you," I asked. "How would you rate your truthfulness as a professional?"

"Look," he leaned back, lifted his arms in a gesture of resignation, "I never represented myself to be a saint. I did what was required. Guy comes into one of my offices and says he wants to buy a house, my people would show him what he needed to do to close the deal. That was it. That was the service I provided."

"May I ask a question?"

"Shoot. I've got nothing to hide."

"When the government showed that your business practices contributed to losses of more than $20 million, did you feel any sense of responsibility?"

"I'm not my brother's keeper," he said. "A man should know what he's getting himself into. If he can't afford the payment, then he shouldn't sign up for it. I don't see why I should be held responsible for anyone else's bad decisions. Caveat emptor."

"But doesn't that same principle of caveat emptor apply to business professionals? Should we also pay attention to what's going on around us and accept responsibility for our own decisions?"

"Of course," Jason said. "Caveat emptor applies to everyone. Let the buyer be aware."

"Then you're agreeing that we all bear responsibility to understand the business we're in?"

Jason nodded his head. "That's right."

"Okay, then explain for me how not knowing about wire fraud or mail fraud should exempt you from responsibility?"

"I'm not a lawyer," he said. "Those sound like legal terms."

"Maybe you're right," I acknowledged. "I didn't know what they meant before my own problems. But in your experience as a real estate professional—a money guy—did you know that your firm was helping people borrow money that they wouldn't be able to repay?"

"Like I said, that wasn't my concern. I was providing a service."

"When seven out of every 10 borrowers defaulted, what did that tell you?"

"It told me that people made irresponsible decisions," Jason admitted.

"So did you have an idea that your firm was arranging loans for a lot of people who wouldn't be capable of repaying them?"

"Everyone was making those loans."

"After arranging the loans, did you use the mail, the telephone, and the Internet to sell those loans to investors— even though you expected the borrowers to default?"

"You make it sound so insidious," Jason told me. "It wasn't as clear as all that."

"But how would you characterize the business? Was it good, honest, and clean, or was it predicated on fraud—on loans that you didn't expect people to repay?"

Chapter Fourteen

"The thing about it was that I never thought of it in terms you're describing," Jason said. "I didn't set out to cheat anyone. The market existed. My wife and I built our business around it."

"That's exactly what I'm trying to help you see. Instead of relying upon strong ethical principles to guide our decisions, we sometimes allowed outside forces—like markets or careers—to blind us from doing what's right. Before we know it, we're enmeshed in deceit without even realizing the harm we cause. That's what happened to me when I finally came to terms with my charges of securities fraud. I'm not judging you in any way. All that I'm trying to show is what I learned. The decisions we make today influence the lives we live tomorrow."

Business people like Jason ignored the far-reaching consequences of their actions at their own peril. Although legal terms like wire fraud and mail fraud may not have been clearly understood, Jason did not dispute that the business he built with his wife was instrumental in issuing mortgage loans that that he expected to default. After collecting fees and commissions, he packaged those loans and sold them into secondary markets, knowing full well that investors would incur losses. He could appease his conscious with claims that he was only providing a service, but when the service was premised on deceit—such as creating pools of worthless debt that he would play a role in selling to investors—willful ignorance would not excuse him from the high and far-reaching costs of a criminal prosecution.

Like many white-collar offenders—including me—Jason had succumbed to temptation and greed. He didn't fully understand the never-ending ways his actions would influence his life or the lives of others. Over the subsequent weeks that preceded his imprisonment I spent more than 20 hours with him and Cindy. Besides doing what I could to prepare them for the challenges ahead, we discussed the importance of honesty, of character, of embracing the concept that we each had a responsibility to work toward becoming better citizens. We could start by considering ethics as an essential part of our decision making process.

Chapter Fourteen Questions

1. What role do ethics play in evaluating market opportunities?

2. How does ethics relate to the concept of caveat emptor?

3. How far should sales professionals go to apprise business partners or clients of risk?

Chapter Fifteen
Albert's Exposure to Bribery Charges

In the early spring of 2010, Mark Whitacre, a former prisoner, friend and mentor sent me information concerning corporate bribery. The case that Mark suggested I learn from concerned SK Foods, one of our nation's largest tomato processors. According to filings in federal court, executives at SK paid bribes to purchasing managers employed by such well-known companies as Frito-Lay, Safeway and Kraft Foods. In exchange for the bribes, the corrupt purchasing managers provided lucrative contracts or confidential information on bids submitted by competitors.

Those criminal complaints, I knew, would derail the personal lives of each defendant. Victims of the corruption would include all shareholders of companies that invested millions to establish brands, and the customers who purchased products that did not receive appropriate quality assurance. The criminal charges concerning SK Foods, for example, included allegations that the company shipped millions of pounds of bulk tomato paste and puree that fell short of basic quality standards; to cover tracks, executives in the complaint falsified documents. The far-reaching corruption resulted in the processing of food for consumers with mold counts high enough to prohibit legitimate sales under federal law.

Chapter Fifteen

A tidbit about the criminal case against SK Foods intrigued me. It described machinations an accomplice would employ to ascertain whether a company executive would be susceptible to bribery. The conspirator would drop a crisp $100 bill on the floor while dining with someone he wanted to bribe. Then he would bend to pick up the bill, saying: "You must have dropped this. Is it yours?" If the target of the bribe said yes, the conspirator considered him receptive to the probability of influence through bribery.

Not long after I learned about the corruption case against SK Foods, I received a phone call from a man who was being investigated for bribery and kickback offenses. His name was Albert, who had a real estate development company with tens of millions in assets. Unfortunately, Albert described for me how everything that he had created— including his residency in the United States— was put into jeopardy because authorities threatened to indict him in a scheme to bribe public officials. Albert's case, along with the case against SK Foods, made clear how companies left themselves vulnerable to criminal charges when they failed to invest sufficiently in ethical training.

After meeting Albert and listening while he described his ongoing struggles with the criminal justice system, I understood that his was the type of story that corporate trainers and human resource managers should share with employees; professors, too, should use such stories to instruct students who were about to enter the professional workforce. Stories like Albert's illustrated the ubiquitous temptations that existed in the marketplace, and they showed the life-changing events that plagued those who abused trust and discretion.

I met Albert early one evening at a restaurant in Long Beach. The familiar shadow of legal troubles darkened his countenance. From the sadness of his expression, his puffy face and the purple hair-thinned veins that spread across his nose and cheeks, I surmised that he had been relying upon alcohol to forget his problems. When Albert spoke, I detected a slight accent of an indistinguishable origin.

"Where are you from?"

"I live in Irvine," Albert responded as if he had been asked the question too many times.

"It's not really relevant but I thought I detected an accent, as if English wasn't your first language."

"I've worked all my life to cover that up. I was born in Poland. My family immigrated to the United States when I was four." Despite attending all of his schooling in the U.S., marrying an American, rearing his three college-aged children in California, and building a thriving business, Albert's lack of U.S. citizenship threatened his deportation to Poland. "I don't know a single person in Poland. I hardly speak the language and I can't read it at all. You may detect a slight accent from my upbringing but I've been speaking English all my life."

"From the size of the business you've built, it's clear that language hasn't been any barrier to success."

"Anyone with a willingness to work can succeed in America. But with success comes risk. The more financial success a man achieves—especially an immigrant—the more that others want to chop him down. If I hadn't been born in Poland I wouldn't be in this mess right now."

"How did you become the target of a criminal investigation?"

Albert's company specialized in developing raw land. He owned bulldozers, excavators, road graders, dump trucks, boom trucks and all of the equipment necessary to convert sagebrush-covered fields into tree-lined neighborhoods. By installing underground utilities, roads, curbs, gutters and sidewalks, his company laid the

183

groundwork that provided housing and employment for thousands of people. The tax revenues such communities generated had a direct influence on municipalities, making it necessary for Albert and his staff to interact closely with local government officials.

"This entire case," Albert explained, "originated because of Jim, the city administrator who presided over a community I was developing a few years ago. Jim had marital problems that escalated when his wife caught him having an affair with his secretary. Those domestic problems led to a corruption investigation by the FBI. Jim's mistress had made statements in court that led to Jim being charged with violations of the Hobbs Act. To lessen his exposure to punishment, Jim started cooperating with the FBI. Now they're investigating my company, specifically looking to see whether I was part of a bribery scheme."

The Hobbs Act, I learned through research, was codified at Title 18 of the United States Code, Section 1951. The law criminalized interference with interstate commerce by "extortion," and it defined extortion as:

> *the obtaining of property from another, with his consent, induced by wrongful use of actual or threatened force, violence, or fear, or under color of official right.*

"How does a city manager's marital infidelity lead to criminal charges for violating the Hobbs Act?" I didn't make the connection.

"He was the city administrator," Albert corrected me, "not the city manager. That position made him a public official, giving him influence over how leaders in the city would allocate funding, over what permits the city would issue, and over what types of financing the city would pursue. Various committees made up of council members and other leaders, including the mayor, would vote to approve major projects after considerable debate. But the city administrator position played an influential role in the prospects of each individual project."

"Okay, I'm following you. Jim could either be a roadblock or a bridge to your project's success."

"Exactly," Albert acknowledged, "and it was in our interest to work with him. We were developing a community in San Bernardino, turning a few hundred acres of red dirt into subdivisions with housing, a medical center, and shopping and office space. Jim worked closely with Tom, one of my engineers. While going over the plans, Jim hinted about the potential he saw in the project, expressing particular interest in a retirement community that was part of the planned development. That's where the problem originated."

"Why was that a problem?"

"Tom perceived Jim's interest as a potential resource for the project and he acted on it. During one of their meetings, Tom showed Jim a set of site plans with the lot divisions mapped out. That version of Tom's plans identified one of the choice lots as being reserved for Jim. When Jim asked what the proposed lot would cost, Tom projected an estimate of its valuation in time—once the community was developed with utilities, roads, curbs, gutters and sidewalks—but Tom pointed out that the lot didn't have much value at the current stage. He offered to issue a deed for the lot to Jim as a gift."

"Was that the bribe?" I asked.

"If it was, Tom didn't know it. As far as he was concerned, he was sowing seeds of good will. Those were good business decisions. Tom's compensation linked directly to his advancing the project and the budget included such expenses to induce key people. Gifting one of the project's proposed lots may have been aggressive, but the cost basis to the project was next to nothing, especially at the early stage. Tom would be offering much higher concessions to anchor tenants in the commercial properties we would be developing down the line. Such allowances were simple big-picture costs we budgeted to see the project through."

"So what was the problem? Were those rules against giving gifts to city managers that had decision-making authority?"

"Not the city manager." Albert corrected me again. "Jim was the city administrator. He didn't even have decision–making authority. The city council and the mayor would vote to make the decisions. All Jim could do was make presentations and respond to questions about how the project would influence the community. He was simply a conduit, an analyst. But Jim told Tom that since he was a public official, he couldn't accept the gift directly. He asked whether Tom might deed the lot to his secretary."

"Was it the woman you said was his mistress?"

"The very same—Tom didn't care who got the deed. Jim said the law wouldn't allow him to receive the deed because he was a public official, but Jim pointed out that his girlfriend was a private citizen, and laws couldn't prohibit us from gifting the deed to her. Tom thought it was a great idea. He had authority over such decisions and not thinking he was doing anything wrong, Tom and he made arrangements to issue the deed to Jim's girlfriend."

Being a land engineer and real estate project developer, neither Tom nor his boss, Albert, understood much about criminal law. Few citizens did. They were not familiar with the implications of Title 18 USC Section 371, "Conspiracy to commit offense or to defraud the United States." Tom may not have given the deed to Jim directly, but when Albert described the story of how Tom agreed to issue the property deed to Jim's girlfriend, I wondered whether the government could construe his act as being part of a conspiracy to defraud the United States.

A different statute could also apply. Title 18 USC, Section 201 describes the crime of "bribery of public officials and witnesses." It holds that:

> *Whoever—directly or indirectly—corruptly gives, offers or promises anything of value to any public official ... with intent to influence any official act ... shall be ... imprisoned for not more than fifteen years.*

"Was Tom expecting anything specific in exchange for gifting the property deed to Jim's girlfriend?" I wondered about a quid pro quo.

"All that Tom would've wanted was good will, an opportunity to be heard and to make a case. Giving gratuities was a part of business and it made good sense. Like I said, at the time that Tom issued the deed, the project was still in the earliest stage of development. Years would pass before the lots would be ready for building."

"Well, one thing must've led to another. How did the government become interested in your company?"

Albert told me that Jim's wife initiated divorce proceedings after she discovered that Jim was betraying her with his secretary. Those domestic problems led divorce attorneys to begin unraveling the ball of string. They deposed Jim's mistress under oath. During the deposition she told the attorneys that Jim had arranged for Tom to deed a piece of property to her, and that she had later deeded the same property to Jim. The property became an issue in Jim's divorce proceedings, and as they turned ugly, Jim's wife fed the federal authorities information that Jim was up to something shady with the property transaction."

"But if Tom gave the property to Jim's girlfriend, and if Tom didn't ask Jim to do anything specific for him, how does the transaction lead to criminal problems?"

"That's what the Hobbs Act was all about." Albert explained how the FBI worked with federal prosecutors to indict Jim for the crime of extortion under Hobbs. To prove his case, the government only had to show that as a public official, Jim received a payment that he wasn't entitled to receive while knowing that Tom made the payment in return for official acts.

"So even though Jim didn't ask anything of Tom, Jim was guilty of extortion simply by receiving the property—even though he received it indirectly from his girlfriend?"

Albert nodded his head, explaining that it was Jim's status as a public official that subjected him to the criminal charges. Government prosecutors didn't need to show any specific agreements between Tom and Jim. Yet Jim made a proposal to the city council that the city issue municipal bonds to finance the project's development and prosecutors would introduce the proposal as evidence of an implied agreement between Jim and Tom.

"That was his role though," Albert insisted. "He was the city administrator, and the city council relied on him to study the project's feasibility. Municipal bond financing would lead to the types of utility installations that would later result in millions of dollars in new tax revenues, better services for the community, more employment, and all types of other benefits for the city. Jim couldn't authorize a single dime of expenditures. All he could do was present findings that would show how the municipal bond financing would influence community development. The property he received wasn't going to have any influence on how members of the city council would vote. The numbers would have to stand on their own."

"I'm sure you're right," I said, "but can I ask a question?"

"I know what's on your mind," Albert nodded, clenching his jaw.

"If Jim wasn't a decision maker, why would Tom have given him a property deed for free?"

"Projects like ours take years in the making. That's because every decision by the city gets made by a committee. Bureaucracy can slow projects down for months, even years. With interest costs, fluctuating market conditions, and other factors, those delays can add millions to a project's overall cost. The company pays for performance," Albert rubbed his temple, "and Tom's compensation would depend on his ability to meet or exceed budgetary targets. At the earliest stage of development, the cost of a few lots here and there didn't amount to more than the cost of a few meals or tickets to the Angels game. But the good will could go a long way toward advancing the project through the red tape. That's all Tom was after—a little access—nothing crazy or inappropriate. It wasn't as if he was buying the city council to disburse public funds."

The business model that Albert described didn't sound nefarious on the surface, at least not to me. It wasn't quite the same as a kickback scheme. Title 18 of the U.S. Code, Section 874, is one of the federal statutes that criminalize kickbacks involving public officials. A kickback scheme provides a more direct link, as the kickback induces an offender to perform (or to refrain from performing) a specific act in direct exchange for hidden compensation. In contrast, according to what Albert told me, Tom was not inducing Jim to violate his duties as a public official when he offered to deed the property. All he wanted was access and fair consideration, as Albert told the story.

Although the financial crimes in which I participated as a stockbroker didn't include public officials, a kickback scheme played a role. While working at UBS, I was one of two stockbrokers of record for the GLT Venture Fund. My trading partner at UBS, Kenneth Sorosky, and I both had reason to believe that Keith Gilabert, the hedge fund manager who ran the GLT Venture Fund was dishonest and misleading his clients. Both Kenneth and I owed a duty to our profession that we ignored. With our clear and convincing evidence that Keith was manipulating his GLT Venture Fund to perpetuate a Ponzi scheme, Kenny and I had a moral, ethical, and legal responsibility to report the fraud. Yet the GLT Venture Fund was generating hundreds of thousands of dollars in trading commissions. Besides that, Keith provided me with thousands of dollars in illegal kickbacks every month in specific exchange for my ignoring his scheme.

Tom's gifting of the property deed that went to Jim (indirectly) lacked that element of underhanded, specific performance that a kickback required. Although the Hobbs Act made it a crime for a public official like Jim to accept payment or something of value that he was not entitled to receive (like a property deed), I could understand how a honest business owner like Albert might lack an awareness of the illegality when he authorized his employer to make such gifts. On the surface—and from Albert's perspective—Tom was making a good business decision by anticipating obstructions to progress and deploying resources effectively. Yet that strategy implied an ignorance of the law, and ignorance would not serve as an effective shield from prosecution or its consequences.

I've spoken with hundreds of white-collar offenders through my work. Although many were consciously and deliberately deceptive (like Kenneth Sorosky, Keith Gilabert, and myself in our securities fraud), too many were sucked into the criminal justice system because of their failure to understand what acts constituted a crime. On occasion I heard stories from executives like Richard, another client of mine who believed that he was setting steps in motion to protect his employer from criminal prosecution of corporate crimes; instead, his incomplete actions resulted in his own felony conviction and prison term.

Richard's case involved violations of the Sherman anti-trust legislation that prohibited collusion. He was a senior executive for a global corporation with numerous divisions and billions in annual revenues. In an effort to advance his career, Richard agreed to accept a temporary assignment as a leader in a different division from the chemical division he had specialized in during the first two decades of his career.

The new division to which Richard transferred was in the business of manufacturing rubber, and it enjoyed the privilege of being one of only three global companies that dominated the world market for rubber. To Richard's dismay, upon his assumption of control in the temporary position, he observed patterns of collusion and price fixing with the conglomerate's two competitors, and he knew the practice violated anti-trust laws. Richard faced a moral dilemma. He did not want to be a party to violating the law, but neither did he want to sabotage his career by reporting to law enforcement the long-standing illegal practices of his colleagues. Instead, Richard made personnel changes and implemented new policies to discontinue the anti-trust violations.

Yet Richard's actions did not go far enough to shield him from prosecution for white-collar crime. Leaders from one of the other two global competitors made a decision to protect that corporation from prosecution. The corporation entered into an immunity agreement with the U.S. Justice Department. In exchange for providing evidence that prosecutors could use against Richard's company and the other company that had been a longstanding partner in the price-fixing conspiracy, prosecutors would not indict the whistle-blowing partner.

Rather than applauding the changes that Richard implemented to stop price-fixing practices during his brief tenure leading the rubber division, Richard became a scapegoat for the corporation when corporate lawyers negotiated a plea agreement with the Justice Department. Richard served several months in federal prison due to corporate crimes that took place during his brief tenure—before he could implement changes that would bring the rubber division into compliance with the law.

Richard's case was but one of numerous examples of white-collar offenders who never suspected that they were breaking criminal laws. His vulnerability to criminal charges materialized because the changes he implemented to phase out price fixing patterns provided indisputable evidence of this involvement—even if that involvement was to discontinue the practice.

In Albert's case, on the other hand, the possible crime was even more abstract. Tom acted on his discretion to gift a property deed to Jim. Despite there not being accusations of bribery of a public official for anything specific, the Hobbs Act made it illegal for Jim to accept anything of value from Tom. Per Jim's request, Tom deeded the property to Jim's mistress. When Jim began cooperating with federal authorities, they began investigating Albert's company and whether he had any culpability in the offense.

The potential prosecution had monumental significance for Albert because of his immigration status. Although he had lived in the United States since childhood as a lawful permanent resident, Albert never went through the official process of obtaining U.S. citizenship. According to Title 8 of the U.S. Code, section 1227:

any alien who is convicted of a crime for
which a sentence of more or longer may be
imposed, is deportable.

If prosecutors found sufficient evidence to indict Albert for having a role in the offense—as a knowing conspirator or otherwise—he would face more than criminal charges; a conviction would result in the government ordering Albert's deportation to Poland, separating him from his family and all that he built in the United States.

The United States Code and the codes of all 50 states provide a menu that includes criminal offenses numbering in the tens of thousands. Although it would be unreasonable to expect business executives to understand all of the ways that their decisions and actions could expose them to criminal problems, businesses that offered their executives opportunities to participate in ethical training would go far toward reducing vulnerabilities to prosecution for white-collar crime, corporate crime, and all of the ancillary problems that accompany entanglements with the criminal justice system.

Chapter Fifteen Questions

1. Why would Albert be vulnerable to criminal prosecution if it was Tom who deeded the property to Jim's mistress?

2. What ethical implications accompanied Tom's agreement to deed a property to Jim's mistress?

3. What responsibility do business leaders have in establishing ethical principles within their corporate cultures?

Epilogue

When people read broadly (including the fine print), I heard a wise man say, they received an education. When they didn't, they received experience instead.

Reading the "fine print" required skills that I didn't have after college or early in my career. Such skills would have endowed me with the ability to learn from reading more than sentences and paragraphs; I also could learn from reading others people's experiences. Being ignorant of such wisdom, I pushed through my career in search of immediate success and without regard for the development of my ethical core. The end was all that was important, and I convinced myself that it would justify the means. If others encountered troubles along their journey, I smugly dismissed them, certain such problems couldn't possibly afflict my career or my life.

That sense of entitlement I had after graduating from USC blocked my insight into the reality that every decision I made would stay with me throughout my career. To a larger extent, decisions would stay with me throughout my life. A sense of entitlement was a form of arrogance, a weakness. At 25 I felt entitled to oversee hundreds of millions as a stockbroker; at 27 I felt entitled to my country club memberships; at 28 I felt entitled to flash Rolex watches, to sport designer suits, to drive high-end BMW sedans.

Epilogue

What did that sense of entitlement get me? It brought the experience of disgrace. It brought the experience of costs that exceeded a million dollars. It brought the experience of a prison term and other consequences that would last a lifetime.

By reading messages that came with the fine print of life, I would have had a better education. I may even have understood enough to pursue lasting values rather than fleeting possessions or outer possessions. Aristotle wrote that dignity did not come through possessions or positions but in deserving them. Such wisdom was beyond my grasp before, but the hard lessons of experience have convinced me that the only real value in life came through the pursuit of virtues such as truth, honesty, integrity, leadership, courage, fairness, transparency, humility, and service to others.

My misguided sense of entitlement deluded me. Because of it, I couldn't grasp that virtues were nothing more than static platitudes when not actively and consciously pursued. To internalize virtues, or to espouse them as personal values, I've since learned, a person had to make commitments and deliberate choices every day. In so doing, the values became a tool, a compass that would guide all decisions.

My life may have no longer included the glitter, but as I took the daily steps—pursuing ethics in motion—I had a deeper sense of internal success and rightness with the world than any possession could provide. Such a pursuit ensured not only the avoidance of experiences that once derailed my life, but it also kept me on the path to becoming a man of good character. Perhaps it would one day make me worthy of the second chance society has so generously bestowed upon me.

To become a man of good character, I've learned that I didn't need to find better values. All I needed was to live faithfully to the values I professed. That was a constant theme I heard through my work with others who were on their way to steel cages and strip searches. We all could express the virtues, but some of us were a bit too ready to attribute those virtues to ourselves. Rather than acting in ways that were consistent with concepts of truth, humility, compassion, leadership, fairness, and so forth, we made decisions in accordance with what we thought we could get away with. And a wicked sense of entitlement sometimes deceived us into believing that we could get away with much more than turned out to be the case.

The truth that I have learned was that although I could not undo the decisions of my past, I could always work to become better. Some would listen to what I had to share, enhancing their education. Others would tune out, as I once did; my hopes were that their reluctance to listen would not lead to bad experiences of their own.

Without exception, every person profiled in the previous pages understood the difference between right and wrong. Some of them even scored highly on corporate ethics evaluations. Yet as I wrote earlier—and as they discovered—it wasn't enough to know the path to an ethical life. A person had to walk that path every day, with every decision. Instead of calculating or plotting decisions based on whether they would deliver immediate success, the wise person understood that true success, lasting success, came when all decisions flowed in harmony with values professed. Such truisms applied not only to our careers, but also to our lives.

People who relied upon their professed values to guide all decisions immunized themselves from the struggles that plagued those of us who were trapped in the criminal justice system. From personal experience, I knew that the struggles did not end with the service of a prison term.

In many ways, prison was the easiest part of the sanction. It was clearly defined, with a beginning and an end. The real challenge was in living with the consequences of a sullied reputation. That was lifelong. Once reputation had been lost, doing good works or making contributions to society would always be diminished by the blemishes of an indelible disgrace.

In my case, I was branded as "the felon." My prison term may have been complete, but I still had to live under the supervision of a probation officer. I could not travel without permission; I could not spend money I earned without authorization; and I would never escape the stigma of my past. Even when my term of supervised release concluded, I would bear the continuing shame of having to explain my criminal history to those with whom I opened personal or professional relationships. Whereas my parents once glowed with pride when they introduced me as their son the baseball player, the successful stockbroker, the USC graduate, now I stood humiliated as they defended me, explaining why I was *still* a good son, deserving of a second chance.

A peculiar indignity came with having to ask for second chances. This book has been part of my ongoing effort to educate students and business executives so they never had to make such requests. By reading about the experiences that other white-collar offenders and I endured, more people may grasp the importance of making values-based decisions.

THE MICHAEL G. SANTOS FOUNDATION

THINK · THRIVE · LEARN · GROW

Justin Paperny serves as executive director of the Michael G. Santos Foundation, a 501(c)(3) non-profit organization that strives to educate at-risk adolescents and to prepare offenders for successful reentry as contributing citizens.

With financial sponsorship from Corporate America, philanthropic organizations, and individuals, the Michael G. Santos Foundation offers literature, seminars, and workshop materials to schools, correctional institutions, and other organizations. Some of the books available include:

- *Lessons From Prison*
- *Ethics in Motion*
- *Gangsters and Thugs: Consequences that Hustlers Pay*
- *My 8,344th Day in Prison*
- *Success! The Straight-A Guide*

Please visit our Web site for more about the resources and services available through the Michael G. Santos Foundation.

www.MichaelGSantosFoundation.org